The
Millennial
Deception

The Millennial Deception

*Angels, Aliens
and the Antichrist*

Timothy J. Dailey

Chosen Books

A Division of Baker Book House Co
Grand Rapids, Michigan 49516

Published by Chosen Books
A division of Baker Book House Company
P.O. Box 6287, Grand Rapids, MI 49516–6287

Printed in the United States of America

Library of Congress Cataloging-in-Publication Data

Dailey, Timothy J., 1953-
    The millennial deception : angels, aliens and the Antichrist / Timothy J. Dailey.
        p.   cm.
    Includes bibliographical references.
    ISBN 0-8007-9233-5 (pbk.)
    1. Eschatology. 2. Antichrist. 3. Eschatology—Biblical teaching. 4. Antichrist—Biblical teaching. 5. Bible—Prophecies. I. Title.
BT876.D29   1995
236—dc20   95-16266

Contents

Introduction:
Nine Peculiar
Aircraft

There are more things in heaven and earth, Horatio,
Than are dreamt of in your philosophy.

Hamlet

I t was one of those days pilots learn to fly for,
with only a few powder puff clouds to disturb
the crystal clear visibility stretching from one
horizon to the other. The date was June 24, 1947, and
pilot Kenneth Arnold was looking for a military C–46
transport that had crashed in the vicinity of Mount
Rainier in Washington State. The victim's families were
offering a five-thousand-dollar reward, a tidy sum in those
days, for the discovery of the downed plane.

Bright sunlight sparkled off the snow on the state's highest peak, towering 14,000 feet in the distance. Arnold was
soaking up the pristine scenery as he scanned the land-

scape for signs of the C–46 wreckage. It was three o'clock in the afternoon, with no indication that a new era of bizarre spiritual phenomena was poised to commence.

Suddenly a bright flash reflected on Arnold's plane. The astonished pilot, assuming he was in dangerous proximity to another plane, prepared to take evasive action. But he could see no other planes in the vicinity. What could have caused the blinding flash? Then he saw them—a chain of what he described later as "nine peculiar aircraft" flying at that moment across the face of Mount Rainier some twenty miles ahead of him.

It was for the veteran pilot an astounding sight. His mind groped to explain what his unbelieving eyes were seeing. What could they be? His first impression was that they were the newly developed jet aircraft just beginning to appear in the skies. But Arnold had never seen aircraft flying so close to mountain peaks, hugging the vertical terrain with an uncanny precision.

As he drew closer the sight became even more baffling. These strange craft lacked wings and tails. Instead, they were round and somewhat smaller in size than a DC–4 aircraft. What's more, Arnold clocked them at a phenomenal speed of more than 1,700 miles per hour as they flew around the mountain at an altitude of 9,500 feet. Curiously the strange craft, despite their velocity, were executing what Arnold described as "flipping, erratic movements" that would be impossible for any known aircraft.

Arnold continued to observe the craft until they disappeared behind nearby Mount Adams. The entire episode took less than three minutes.

At first his mind attempted to discount the incredible scene he had just witnessed. He continued his search for the downed C–46, increasingly troubled by the strange flying disks. Later, back on the ground, he reported the incident. But none of the suggested explanations, from secret military aircraft to guided missiles, could account for what he had witnessed.

A reporter for Associated Press filed a story about Arnold's experience in which the crafts were said to resemble "flying saucers." The age of UFOs had dawned.

What was perhaps the most puzzling aspect of the experience would continue to haunt Arnold. The remarkable craft, flying more than twenty miles distant from him, seemed to be reacting psychically to his observation of them. In his own words, "Two or three of them every few seconds would dip or change their course slightly, just enough for the sun to strike them at an angle that reflected on my plane."[1]

This seemingly impossible feat for aircraft flying in tandem at high speeds gave Arnold an eerie impression that whoever or whatever was controlling those disks knew he was observing them from a considerable distance and was, in some unfathomable way, *directly engaging his awareness of them.*

So it is that, at the onset of the 1947 UFO flap, there were already indications that paranormal forces beyond our three-dimensional world are involved.

Arnold's experience, which heralded a worldwide fascination with UFOs, intersects with other, seemingly unrelated but equally remarkable events unfolding on the other side of the globe.

That very year, 1947, marked the final, ineffectual attempt of the United Nations to impose a solution on the "Palestine problem." By year's end civil war had broken out between Arabs and Jews, followed by the British decision to abandon their mandate for Palestine. On the same day in which the British High Commissioner for Palestine sailed from Jaffa—May 14, 1948—the Jews declared the sovereign state of Israel.

While there is obviously no direct connection between these far-flung events, it is nonetheless significant that the intervening decades have seen an extraordinary explosion of paranormal activity. The current surge of interest in angelic visitations is often associated (as you may know) with the darker side of terror-inspiring "aliens." An ominous thread runs through such occult phenomena—that of a subliminal preparation for overt spiritual manifestations of a far greater magnitude.

Meanwhile, events no less supernatural continue to unfold in the Middle East, leading many observers to conclude that the stage is being set for the final end-time confrontation between God and the forces of evil, known to students of biblical prophecy as the battle of Armageddon. Perhaps even now the mysterious leader of those forces, known as the Antichrist, stands behind the scenes.

The book of Revelation states that this infamous worldwide leader will command formidable spiritual forces. Is it possible he will preside over such mind-boggling events as the appearance—in full view of an awestruck humanity—of alien "messengers" from outer space?

So it is that I write this book about an alarming spiritual deception abroad in our world. It is an account of demonic subterfuge of a previously unimaginable magnitude waiting to be unleashed on the planet.

Our story will begin with the baffling report of a geologist's drill-hole to hell. Did this weird incident originate on the pages of some supermarket tabloid or did it really happen? Could it be a portent of coming judgment?

The plot thickens as we examine what appears to be the increasing intrusion of "spirit entities," both angelic and demonic, into our world. As we do, let me encourage you to note a progression from the apparently innocent act of picking up hitchhikers, to Betty Eadie being taken for a ride by her "guardian angels," to Whitley

Strieber and other "abductees" being dragged kicking and screaming into a macabre netherworld.

Behind all these strange phenomena is a subtle attempt by our spiritual adversary to condition our world for the acceptance of a new spiritual reality. When viewed in the light of the Bible, however, the innocuous-sounding New World Order bears an unmistakable resemblance to the final rebellion against God led by the Antichrist. Accordingly, we will focus our attention on this mysterious personage and examine some intriguing candidates from the halls of history and our own time.

Last but certainly not least, we will explore how to effectively resist the insidious spiritual offensive that is already underway, and how we can be among those spoken of in the book of Revelation who "overcame [Satan] by the blood of the Lamb and by the word of their testimony" (Revelation 12:11).

Secular UFO researchers have theorized that the alien invasion already upon us cannot be hostile in the first-order sense of the word. Otherwise, as Jacques Vallee speculates, with their massively superior technology "they could have taken over our planet a long time ago."[2] As we shall see, however, it could simply be a matter of timing.

One thing is apparent: We are already witnessing a masterful satanic subterfuge that appears to involve the appearance of "angels" and "aliens." Many are asking whether the coming of the Antichrist can be far removed. From the Bible we learn that such an evil day surely lies ahead. The question for our consideration, then, is this: Are we in the throes of that final otherworldly deception *now?*

Part 1

Rumors
of Angels

1

A Bat
Out of Hell

It was a bizarre news report squeezed between the usual disturbing coverage of the day's violence in the ongoing Palestinian *intifada*. We were living on the West Bank near Bethlehem at the time and, not having a television set, missed the story. The report apparently did not reach the Western press. Israeli television, however, aired it. Our pastor, who saw the broadcast, told us the gist of what appeared to be an amazing encounter with unearthly spiritual entities: A ghastly demonic being was reported to have escaped from a Siberian drill site.

What is one supposed to make of such a story? It fit into the same category as the Loch Ness monster and the abominable snowman—reports that are never quite backed up by indisputable evidence. So it was filed away in some mental *Titillating Rumors* file and promptly forgotten. But it did not go away.

A few years later my family and I moved to Haifa, Israel's third largest city, situated on Mount Carmel overlooking the Mediterranean Sea. One day while having a discussion with some friends of ours from New Zealand about spiritual phenomena, I happened to mention the Siberian drill site story as a candidate for my tall tales file.

"Yes," they beamed. They knew all about the story.

"Right," replied I. "I'll bet you do."

"We have a news article about it," countered our friends.

"You have a *what?*" I exclaimed.

They went running and came back with a photocopied article from the *Weekly World News* dated April 24, 1990. Due to the riveting nature of the account, I will quote extensively from the article, entitled "Scientists Dig 9-Mile-Deep Hole and Claim: 'We Drilled through the Gates of Hell.'"[1] See what *you* think of it:

> Scientists who drilled a nine-mile hole to study the movements of massive plates under the Earth's surface claim to have discovered hell. That is the word from the respected Finnish newspaper *Ammenusastia*, which quoted Soviet geologist Dmitri Azzacov as saying that a terrifying winged creature flew out of the hole before microphones were lowered— revealing the screams of the damned.
>
> "As a Communist I don't believe in heaven or the Bible but as a scientist I now believe in hell," said Dr. Azzacov.
>
> "Needless to say we were shocked to make such a discovery. But we know what we saw and we know what we heard. And we are absolutely convinced that we drilled through the gates of hell."

Both the name and photograph of the (then) Soviet geologist appeared in the story, along with photographs of the alleged technicians and drill site. The article continues:

The terrifying drama reportedly unfolded when the Soviet geologists, drilling at an unspecified site in western Siberia, reached a depth of nine miles.

According to Dr. Azzacov, "the drill suddenly began to rotate wildly, indicating we had reached a large empty pocket or cavern.

"Temperature sensors showed a dramatic increase in heat to 2,000 degrees Fahrenheit." At this point in the account a seemingly fantastic event takes place, as described by Dr. Azzacov:

"When we raised the drill we couldn't believe our eyes. A fanged creature with huge evil eyes appeared in a gaseous cloud and shrieked like a wild animal before it disappeared. Some workers and technicians fled but those of us who remained were determined to learn more. We lowered a microphone, designed to detect the sounds of plate movements down the shaft."

As if the sight of the demonic were not enough, the remaining technicians would reportedly soon hear blood-curdling sounds:

"But instead of plate movements we heard a human voice screaming in pain. At first we thought that the sound was coming from our own equipment.

"But when we made adjustments our worst suspicions were confirmed. The screams weren't those of a single human, they were the screams of millions of humans. Luckily, we had the recorder going and we have the nightmarish sounds on tape.

"At that point we suspended the project and capped the hole. It was obvious that we had discovered something beyond our comprehension. We had seen and heard things that were never meant to be seen and heard."

The *Weekly World News* article said that Soviet officials refused to comment on the report pending the review of the tapes and the completion of an investigation. The

Finnish newspaper *Ammenusastia* concluded in a page-one editorial that "the world has a right to know" what happened at the Siberian drill site.

The article seemed almost too good to be true. And it was: I learned that the *Weekly World News* is a supermarket tabloid. It appears in the checkout lane next to its literary cousins boldly proclaiming scoops such as *Twelve U.S. Senators Are Space Aliens!*

Case closed? Surprisingly, not quite.

While in Haifa I had the privilege of teaching theology to Russian Jewish believers in Jesus who had recently immigrated to Israel. During one of our discussions, I happened to bring up the Siberian story as an example of unfounded religious claims, asking in passing if any of them were familiar with it.

To my surprise, they not only knew all about it, but assured me it was widely held to be true by Christians in Russia. To a person they had seen reports in the Russian media about the remarkable incident. Christians had, in fact, made copies of the articles to use as an evangelistic tool.

By now I was baffled. The only other news report I could find on the subject was a tongue-in-cheek treatment of the incident in *Christianity Today* by talk-show host Rich Buhler,[2] who said nothing about the reports in the Russian media that my students spoke of.

So What about It?

What are we to make of stories about demons escaping from drill holes? Let's examine two possibilities.

1. The story is a hoax. I must admit that the report is so startling that I hesitated to pass it on, especially since the only hard copy I have comes from a supermarket tabloid of dubious credibility. But one nagging fact remained: My Russian students—mature adults from various parts of the Soviet Union—knew about the story from the Russian press *before* the story appeared in the West.

That is to say, while I cannot vouch for the veracity of the *Weekly World News* or even its source, the Finnish newspaper *Ammenusastia,* the question is moot because the story *antedates* both of them. Also worth mentioning is the fact that the story was broadcast on Israeli state-run television and may have been seen in other European countries. It is doubtful that Israeli television or any respectable news organization would broadcast a story they knew to be wholly unfounded, although it is possible that they aired the story without verifying the sources.

Furthermore, the account was believed to be true not only by my Russian immigrant students but by many other Christians in Russia. Which raises a question: If the story was an elaborate hoax, what possible motivation would self-proclaimed atheistic geologists have in perpetrating it? The same objection applies regarding its fabrication by the Russian press.

2. Something extraordinary actually occurred at the Siberian test site. Before we consider this possibility, let's see if the Bible has anything to say about such phenomena.

Interestingly, the book of Revelation records a similar future event. In chapter nine a "star" (likely an angelic being) is given "the key to the shaft of the Abyss" (verse 1):

> When he opened the Abyss, smoke rose from it like the smoke from a gigantic furnace. . . . And out of the smoke locusts came down upon the earth and were given power like that of scorpions of the earth.
>
> Revelation 9:2–3

These demonic creatures resembled battle horses:

> On their heads they wore something like crowns of gold,
> and their faces resembled human faces. Their hair was like
> women's hair, and their teeth were like lions' teeth. . . . They
> had as king over them the angel of the Abyss, whose name
> in Hebrew is Abaddon, and in Greek, Apollyon.
>
> verses 7–8, 11

Note that the location of the demonic underworld, called the Abyss (other translations render it *bottomless pit*), is described as being somewhere underneath the surface of the earth. Revelation 11:7 and 17:8 confirm this, stating that the Beast "*comes up* from the Abyss."

The Siberian drill shaft episode obviously cannot be said to fulfill this specific prophecy in the book of Revelation. It does, however, bear curious resemblance to the biblical account of demonic beings escaping from the Abyss.

But why would God allow a demonic creature to escape from the Abyss in full view of geologists and technicians? The answer might be found, in part, in the fact that copies of the Siberian drill shaft story were widely distributed and used by Christians in Russia as an evangelistic tool and as a graphic confirmation of the truthfulness of the Bible.

Here is a possibility worth considering: God, in His divine sovereignty, permitted this remarkable event at precisely this juncture in the history of the fragmented former Soviet Union. The demise of atheistic Marxist-Leninism had left a gaping spiritual hole in the hearts and minds of the world's largest country. After being told for seventy years that God and the supernatural do not exist, the philosophy of atheism was at long last exposed for the bankrupt system it is. Russia finds herself at a spiritual crossroads perhaps as never before. Did God allow this supernatural incident to occur as a sobering testimony to the Russian people about spiritual realities?

Since the Siberian drill shaft story has to date been neither proven nor discredited, two extremes should be
avoided. The first is the unfortunate tendency among
prophecy teachers to pass along such fascinating reports
to their audiences uncritically as if they were demonstra-
bly true. This may be due to their inadvertent but nonetheless shrewd realization that audiences are flocking to hear
just this kind of thing. The apostle Paul warns:

> The time will come when men will not put up with sound
> doctrine. Instead, to suit their own desires, they will gather
> around them a great number of teachers to say what their
> itching ears want to hear.
>
> 2 Timothy 4:3

This failure to discern truth from error may have the
short-term effect of gluing the audience to their seats,
but will result in the long run in prophecy burnouts—
jaded Christians who, having been disillusioned time and
again by sensationalist claims, want nothing more to do
with the subject. This is a regrettable and all-too-common consequence that prophecy teachers would do well
to consider before they gear up to "tickle the ears" of
their audiences.

The other extreme to be avoided is the knee-jerk dis-
counting of all reports of supernatural phenomena. The
great danger here is succumbing inadvertently to the
relentlessly anti-Christian and antisupernatural mindset
that holds sway over our culture. It can scarcely be
ignored: The offensive against Christianity is gaining
momentum in Western culture, and we need to ask ourselves: *Am I really clear about which side I am on in this
battle?* Even if many such reports do turn out to be bogus,
we must not join the ranks of the scorners, but continue
to hold open the possibility of divine intervention in our
world.

Indeed, such intervention is not only conceivable but *inevitable*:

> First of all, you must understand that in the last days scoffers will come, scoffing and following their own evil desires. They will say, "Where is this 'coming' he promised? Ever since our fathers died, everything goes on as it has since the beginning of creation." . . . But do not forget this one thing, dear friends: With the Lord a day is like a thousand years, and a thousand years are like a day. The Lord is not slow in keeping his promise, as some understand slowness. He is patient with you, not wanting anyone to perish, but everyone to come to repentance.
>
> 2 Peter 3:3–4, 8–9

Conclusion

Let us summarize what we can learn, then, from the Siberian drill site story. First, until such reports are established beyond reasonable doubt, we should treat them as unconfirmed. It is important to remember that if such accounts turn out to be false, it in no way implies that our faith is also invalid. The truth claims of the Bible and Christianity do not depend on the accuracy of any questionable present-day occurrences.

Second, if over a period of time the story should gain a measure of veracity, we can view this remarkable event as a divine warning about both the reality of evil spiritual forces and the horror of eternal separation from God. That is something for each of us to consider.

I have chosen this bizarre story as our first example of the unusual spiritual phenomena being reported in our day. The accounts we shall examine are controversial, and we shall investigate the pros and cons of each incident. In the end you must decide for yourself whether a genuine manifestation of otherworldly power actually took place.

With this in mind, we now plunge into a mysterious netherworld of seductive spirit beings and fearsome aliens. We begin with reports of angelic hitchhikers on darkened roads. Other spirits—or are they of the same order?—take a woman from her hospital bed, also in the night. And from there we descend to the unthinkable.

2

Highway Hallucinations or Angelic Messengers?

The account of the unbelievable occurrences spread through the hushed, college-age Bible study with electrifying effect. The time was the height of the Jesus People movement in the early 1970s when a far-reaching spiritual revival was sweeping the youth of America. God's power was being manifest in miraculous ways. The weekly Bible study had mushroomed until those in attendance filled every square foot of the living room. Tonight we listened in rapt attention as the visiting speaker related an extraordinary phenomenon reported in several areas of the country that defied rational explanation.

With minor variations, the accounts went like this: A
person or persons are driving in their car, usually at night

and typically through a rural area. Their automobile head-lights illuminate a hitchhiker on the road ahead. Unaccustomed to picking up strangers, they pass him by and continue on their way.

Some time later they see another hitchhiker up ahead, waiting for a ride with thumb outstretched. Drawing closer, they note a resemblance to the previous hitchhiker. *It couldn't be!* Unnerved, they drive past.

By now their sense of isolation, heightened by traveling through a remote area at night, is beginning to register. They continue warily on. Sure enough, several miles later, yet another figure is seen in the distance, standing motionless on the gravel shoulder. Not daring to stop, they see to their alarm that he bears an uncanny resemblance to the others passed up earlier.

The inevitable happens. As they scan the road ahead anxiously, the headlights pick out in the distance yet another hitchhiker. This time, finally convinced they are destined to stop, they pull over to the side of the road.

The hitchhiker climbs into the back of the car, sometimes described as neat and well-dressed, sometimes marked by his long hair and blue jeans as a "hippie" (the slang term for the youth of the counterculture movement in their radical rejection of the conservative status quo). A conversation ensues that turns to spiritual matters. At some point the hitchhiker makes a simple affirmation, "Jesus is coming again soon," and then—hold onto your seats—*disappears* from the car!

The effect of these accounts upon our young minds at a time of spiritual awakening can scarcely be exaggerated. For us it was not only possible but probable in the light of what we believed about the soon coming of Jesus Christ.

With the passing of time, however, the strange reports ceased and we gradually forgot about the disappearing hitchhiker. But it was, oddly enough, a story that would not go away.

Years later, in 1980, a UPI report appeared in the respectable, Midwest, cornbelt *Indianapolis Star* describing the same baffling phenomenon:

> Little Rock (UPI)—Reports of a mysterious hitchhiker who talks about the second coming of Jesus Christ and then disappears into thin air from moving cars has sparked the imagination of highway travelers and mystified the Arkansas State Police.
>
> "It sure is a weird story," Trooper Robert Roten said Friday.
>
> Roten said the state police have had two reports—both on a Sunday—that a clean-cut, well-dressed hitchhiker has disappeared from cars traveling along highways near Little Rock.[1]

The reporter writing the story was unable to locate anyone who actually saw the disappearing act. He found no lack of individuals, however, who had heard about the mystery hitchhiker:

> One such woman, who emphasized she could not verify the story, heard about the hitchhiker from a woman she rides to work with. That woman had heard it from another woman whose parents supposedly were involved in the incident. Lowering her voice, the woman told the story thus:
>
> "The girl said her parents and another couple were coming from Pine Bluff. They picked up this neatly dressed man because he looked like he needed transportation, you know. He discussed current events—he knew all about the hostages—and all of a sudden he said, 'Jesus Christ is coming again' and disappeared.
>
> "They stopped the first trooper they saw and told him, 'You're going to think we're crazy' and told him about it. And he said, 'No, you're the fourth party that's told me about it today.'"

An investigation revealed that two police reports had indeed been filed one week apart in the summer of 1982:

> Roten said he checked with police districts all over the state and found only the two reports in Little Rock. One was logged June 29 by a woman who said the man had disappeared from her car while driving on U.S. 65 between Pine Bluff and Little Rock. The other was July 6 from a man who said it happened to friends of his on Interstate 30 between Benton and Little Rock.
>
> "There's not much we can do on a report like that," Roten said. "It's not a violation of the law and no hazard is involved. It's illegal to hitchhike, but if he disappears, this hitchhiker is going to be hard to arrest."

Are They Angels?

Here we go again! What are we to make of these spooky reports about angelic hitchhikers? Is it possible that God sends angels to stand alongside roads for the purpose of announcing the Second Coming of His Son?

The Bible does not, so far as I can tell, deny that such manifestations *can* take place. After all, the very word *angel* in both Hebrew and Greek means "messenger." We are all familiar with Bible stories in which angels were used as messengers, perhaps most notably in the annunciation to Mary concerning the birth of the Messiah.

And lest we forget, we actually have an account of a disappearing hitchhiker in the New Testament: the story of Philip and the Ethiopian eunuch in Acts 8. The eunuch stopped to pick up Philip, who proclaimed the Gospel to him. After they had stopped for an impromptu baptism, "the Spirit of the Lord suddenly took Philip away, and the eunuch did not see him again" (Acts 8:39).

But can angels be expected to appear and disappear today? A surprising number of people think so. According to a recent *Time* magazine survey, 69 percent of those polled believe in the existence of angels; and fully one-third claimed to have felt an angelic presence personally in their lifetime.[2] Capitalizing on the current fascination with such phenomena, books like Sophy Burnham's bestseller *A Book of Angels* describe modern-day spectral visitations that have allegedly occurred. We will look at one such account in detail in the next chapter. But for the present let's return to our Arkansas angelic hitchhiker story.

The wire article states that two reports from June and July 1982 came from police files, indicating at least two cases in which individuals experienced *something* (leaving aside for the moment the possibility of outright fabrication) that caused them to go to the police in the first place. Unfortunately, the sole witness interviewed in the article could provide only a thirdhand account. By that time, whatever actually took place could have been greatly embellished and would scarcely hold up in a court of law.

This is not to say that this particular report was false. On the other hand, we cannot know for certain that a supernatural angelic visitation actually took place. Until such verification is forthcoming, such reports should not be passed on as if they were proven (as occurred, for example, in my Bible study in the early '70s).

In his book *The Vanishing Hitchhiker,* Professor Jan Harold Brunvand of the University of Utah offers another explanation for this phenomenon. Brunvand catalogs what he refers to as "urban myths," stories that have arisen in popular American folk culture and that continue to surface in varied forms over the passage of time. He considers the vanishing hitchhiker stories, which he traces over a period of some forty years, to be a prime example of what he calls "classic automobile legends."

One variant of the vanishing hitchhiker legend, according to Brunvand, includes an apocalyptic pronouncement:

Another major development in the long and complex history of the roadside ghost is almost predictable, given the nature of folklore and the changing times. Lydia M. Fish of the State University of New York at Buffalo discovered in more than sixty texts she and her students collected locally that the current hitchhiker is likely to be "a beautiful young hippie clad in shining white" who engages his host or hosts in a conversation about Jesus and His Second Coming before disappearing. Sometimes he even leaves his seat belt buckled up.[3]

One of the stories Brunvand recounts dates from 1972 and was told by a nineteen-year-old man from Amherst, New York, a suburb of Buffalo:

> My friend John Hogan, who I went to DeSalles High with, told me this. He goes to St. John Fisher College now. His fiancée and her aunt, who's a nun, were going down the Thruway and they picked this hitchhiker up at the entrance. They were coming from Syracuse and going to Rochester. The guy wanted to know if they had ever heard the gospel and if they knew Jesus. Then he'd go, "He's coming soon" and then next thing they knew he was gone.

Up until this point there were only two people involved, John Hogan's fiancée and her aunt. The lack of witnesses to the vanishing hitchhikers is, on the one hand, frustrating, and on the other hand to be expected due to the nature of the phenomenon. How many witnesses, after all, can squeeze into one automobile? But in this incident, look what happens next:

> They stopped at the nearest service area, pulled up to the gas station attendant and rolled down the window to report it. They were pretty shook up and felt kind of dumb. The guy said he wasn't surprised and would they believe about twenty other people had reported the same story. . . . My

father works as a toll collector at the Williamsville Thruway entrance and he heard a lot about it.[4]

Brunvand attempts to reduce the vanishing hitchhiker phenomenon to a modern American myth. But just as it is difficult to verify these reports, so it is difficult to dismiss them. In the final analysis, the matter rests with the veracity of the witnesses.

As for Brunvand's contention that the phenomenon is a distinctly American urban myth, it would seem that the vanishing hitchhikers are world travelers, as indicated by the following report from West Germany. The year is 1982, ten years after the story of the young man from near Buffalo. The following UPI article appeared, once again, in the *Indianapolis Star*:

> Rosenheim, West Germany (UPI)—Police say they are on the watch for a "ghost" hitchhiker who claimed to be the Archangel Gabriel and who unnerved several motorists by predicting a 1984 Doomsday before he vanished from moving cars.
>
> The first reported sighting of the so-called archangel happened Tuesday when a 30-year-old woman picked up a hitchhiker in blue jeans carrying a knapsack on the Munich-Salzburg superhighway.
>
> Police said the hitchhiker told the woman he was the "Archangel Gabriel." They said he prophesied the end of the world in 1984 and then suddenly disappeared from her moving car, even though he was strapped in by a seatbelt.
>
> They said the woman claimed the hitchhiker's seatbelt was still locked after he disappeared. Since then "more than half a dozen" motorists had notified authorities of similar appearances.
>
> A police spokesman said, "We are looking for this person or 'archangel' but his tendency to suddenly vanish is complicating the search."[5]

The discerning reader will note the year of this wire story, 1982, and realize that, whatever happened on the German autobahn, it was not an angel sent from God. How do we know this? Through the benefit of hindsight. Up until December 31, 1984, it would have been possible for this to be a true prediction announced by a divine messenger. But since doomsday did not occur in 1984, and since this statement did not appear as a conditional, Nineveh-like prophecy ("*If* you do not repent . . ."), and since God does not send His angels on missions of deceit, we are left with two possible explanations.

First, that the series of reported incidents were a fabrication, or perhaps some kind of misguided hysteria that inflamed people's imaginations.

Yet a significant number of reports—"more than half a dozen"—would require at least that many people willing to take the time and effort to go to the police with their phony stories. Possible, but who would be interested in perpetrating such a deception? Evangelical Christians, the very people most interested in the Second Coming, would presumably be the *least* likely to lie to the police. Similarly, the occurrence of a half-dozen reports throws doubt upon the hysteria option. While we can easily imagine a single disturbed individual claiming that an angel disappeared from his or her moving car, it is considerably less plausible that at least six different people suffered from the same hallucination.

There is a second possibility: Something indeed happened on the Munich-Salzburg autobahn in 1982, but it was not an angel of God that appeared—or disappeared. Could this "archangel Gabriel" have been a demonic manifestation? It is a possibility worth considering, even though some in the Church think it is unspiritual to question reports of miraculous events, let alone suggest that the source might actually be demonic.

There can be no doubt, however, as to our responsibility in this realm: "Dear friends, do not believe every spirit, but test the spirits to see whether they are from God, because many false prophets have gone out into the world" (1 John 4:1).

Why is it necessary to test the spirits? Surely it would be obvious which side such a being is on? Unfortunately it is not obvious, for these demonic impersonators are masters of deception and of cleverly disseminating false teaching. The apostle Paul warned, "But even if we or *an angel from heaven* should preach a gospel other than the one we preached to you, let him be eternally condemned!" (Galatians 1:8, italics mine).

In these days of heightened prophetic speculation, many are being led astray (as will become increasingly clear) by deceiving, manipulative spirit beings. We must remember that the devil also has his "angels" (Matthew 25:41).

But here is another puzzling question: Why would the evil one want to advertise the manifestly true proclamation *Jesus is coming again*? One answer lies in the fact that, at least in the German autobahn case, the message was subtly different. The "angel" specifically—and falsely—prophesied the end of the world in 1984. When 1984 came and went, that "prophecy" could be used only to discredit those who believe in the Second Coming, like Aesop's shepherd boy who repeatedly cried "Wolf!" until no one believed him when the wolf actually showed up.

Conclusion

Let's summarize our analysis of the angelic hitchhiker phenomenon. First, we should not reject out-of-hand the possibility that such an event can occur in the providence of God, lest we fall into the antisupernatural bias of our age. Second, since the reports of mystery hitchhikers tend to be either secondhand or almost impossible to verify, they should not be spread abroad as if they are true beyond any doubt. Third, we must be on guard against satanic deceptions and false prophecies that aim to bring into disrepute teaching and preaching about biblical prophecy.

We began our investigation into recent spiritual phenomena with reported demons from oil wells; now we have seen "angels" in the back seats of cars. We will now look at a well-known example.

3

Entertaining Angels Unawares

I t is a story so captivating, written in such a straightforward, unaffected manner, that it soared despite its controversial subject matter to the top of the *New York Times* bestseller list. Billed as "the most profound and complete near-death experience ever," Betty J. Eadie's story is really about angels—the beings of light that shepherded her on her intriguing journey to the afterworld.

Her book *Embraced by the Light* appears at first reading to be a quaint but harmless vision of heaven. A closer examination, however, raises serious questions about the nature of her experience.

Eadie's story actually took place nineteen years earlier as she lay in the hospital one evening recuperating from a routine operation. In a chapter with the arresting title "My Death," she relates how her body suddenly grew weaker and weaker. Her fears became magnified with the sense that something was going terribly wrong. Attempting to reach the cord to summon the nurse, she found she was unable to move.

What follows is a textbook case of what is known as an out-of-body experience and astral projection, both of which are associated with occultism. And while Betty Eadie's religious experience seems worlds apart from occultism, it is not long before we encounter disturbing aspects of her story.

As Eadie describes it, all at once she felt a *pop* as her spirit was drawn out of her body. She found herself floating near the ceiling and looking down at her motionless form on the bed. She felt no pain or regret, only a sense of awe. Then she realized she was not alone. Three men dressed in brown robes appeared at her side whom she recognized as her "choicest friends." Later she describes them as her guardian angels.

Her story has barely begun when we discover a major theological difficulty with the book: It is replete with references to the preexistence of souls. The three angels inform her they have been with her "for eternities," to which Eadie explains her reaction:[1]

> I didn't fully understand this; I had a difficult time comprehending the concept of eternity, let alone eternities. Eternity to me had always been in the future, but these beings said they had been with me for eternities in the past.
>
> page 32

In explaining herself, Eadie inadvertently gives the reason the Christian Church has rejected belief in the preexistence of souls: If souls have lived for "eternities in the past," and will live for eternity in the future, they possess a fundamental aspect of God's own nature—His eternality.[2] The Bible teaches clearly that only God has existed from eternity past. For example:

Before the mountains were born or you brought forth the
earth and the world, from everlasting to everlasting you are
God.

Psalm 90:2

Mankind is a created being and does not share in God's
eternality. It is true that eternal life is the wondrous gift
of God to all who believe, but this refers to our living with
Him forever, not to any supposed eternal preexistence.
Those who reject Jesus Christ as Lord and Savior, on the
other hand, have no hope of eternal life: "Whoever
believes in the Son has eternal life, but whoever rejects
the Son will not see life, for God's wrath remains on him"
(John 3:36).

These biblical truths are conspicuously missing from
Eadie's upbeat version of the afterlife, which projects a
vastly different scenario from the one predicted by Jesus
when He warned that "broad is the road that leads to
destruction, and many enter through it" (Matthew 7:13).

Another Jesus

But let's continue with Betty Eadie's account of her after-
death experience. After a quick astral projection trip home
to check on her family, she is drawn at fantastic speed
through a dark tunnel with an increasingly radiant light
at the end. That light, it turns out, is none other than Jesus:

> It was the most unconditional love I have ever felt, and as I
> saw his arms open to receive me, I went to him and received
> his complete embrace and said over and over, "I'm home.
> I'm home. I'm finally home." I felt his enormous spirit and
> knew that I had always been a part of him, that in reality I
> had never been away from him. And I knew that I was wor-
> thy to be with him, to embrace him.

page 41

While in the presence of this spirit being that she calls Jesus, Eadie is invited to ask him about anything on her mind. Her questions follow one after another in rapid succession. She discovers that she has immediate comprehension so that she can "understand volumes in an instant." In fact, Eadie describes her new ability in terms usually reserved for God:

> The word "omniscient" had never been more meaningful to me. Knowledge permeated me. In a sense it *became* me, and I was amazed at my ability to comprehend the mysteries of the universe simply by reflecting on them.
>
> page 45

At first Eadie refers to her Jesus as God, a confession possibly intended to ease the concerns of Christians about her experience. The divinity of Jesus is, after all, a key confessional belief of Christianity. Before long, however, another concept of Jesus emerges. We are informed that, instead of being God incarnate, Jesus is "a God" (p. 44). Does this mean there are other "Gods" in the universe? Although Eadie claims near-omniscient ability to understand the mysteries of the universe, this basic question either escapes her notice or remains unaddressed.

Unfortunately, only a few other scraps can be gleaned from the text to help the reader understand the nature of Eadie's Jesus, and what we learn only raises more questions. We are told, for example, that Eadie's "Protestant upbringing" had apparently misled her into believing that "God the Father and Jesus Christ were one being":

> I understood, to my surprise, that Jesus was a separate being from God, with his own divine purpose, and I knew that God was our mutual Father.
>
> page 47

Elsewhere she speaks of each individual's "divine, spiritual nature" (p. 50).

But if, as she claims, God is the mutual Father of Jesus and the rest of humanity, Jesus becomes just another spirit being on a level with others that Eadie encounters on her journey. I hesitate to criticize Betty Eadie's book because she gives the impression of being a sincere woman of strong faith, and *Embraced by the Light* contains many commendable reflections. But something vitally important is at stake here: the historic Christian affirmation of the uniqueness of Jesus Christ.

According to the Bible, Jesus is nothing less than God the Son, the second Person of the Trinity. He Himself said, "I and the Father are one" (John 10:30). History has shown that when the divine uniqueness of Jesus is taken away, there remains little reason to proclaim the Christian faith, and all religions become equally valid.

Indeed, when Betty Eadie asks "Jesus" why there are so many different religions, she is told that "all religions on the earth are necessary because there are people who need what they teach" (p. 45). The message is unmistakable: Christians must not consider their religion as truer than any other:

> Having received this knowledge, I knew that we have no right to criticize any church or religion in any way. They are all precious and important in his sight. Very special people with important missions have been placed in all countries, in all religions. . . .
>
> page 46

The implications of this are momentous: The inhumanity of the Hindu caste system, paganism, witchcraft and untold religious systems are equally "precious and important."

Are we to believe that God approves of religions that do not bow the knee to Jesus Christ as Savior and Lord, religions that have kept untold masses in spiritual bondage and whose beliefs contradict what Jesus Himself taught? These words of Eadie's Jesus constitute nothing less than a rejection of the words of Jesus Christ as found in the New Testament: "I am the way and the truth and the life. No one comes to the Father except through me" (John 14:6).

There are not manifold ways of salvation (despite an increasing movement in the West toward religious pluralism) any more than there are many answers to the mathematical addition of two plus two. Either Jesus is the eternal Truth or, as in Betty Eadie's heavenly scenario, He takes His place among the ranks of the rest of us.

Heaven's Industrial Zone

As we continue, increasingly wary, on our journey through Betty Eadie's otherworldly experience, we find that the bulk of the teachings revealed to her find little support in the New Testament.

The more we learn about her heaven, in fact, the more suspicious it becomes. Eadie is taken to a workshop where people are "weaving on large, ancient-looking looms." She admits her surprise as to the presence of such archaic devices in the spirit world, and is told that the fabric is made into clothing for those newly arrived in the spirit world.

We are surprised along with her, for we were told earlier that the spirit world is the creative source behind human technology:

Many of our important inventions and even technological developments were first created in the spirit by spirit prodigies. Then individuals on earth received the inspiration to create these inventions here.

page 48

If the spirit world is the inspiration for our modern inventions, why are the spirits themselves laboring away (albeit voluntarily) with backward, primitive devices? In addition, there is something more than a little curious about the notion of a heavenly sweatshop for spirit clothing.

As Eadie continues her tour of heaven's industrial zone, she is shown "a large machine, similar to a computer, but much more elaborate and powerful" (pp. 74–75). Those working on this machine show her their work, although in this case we are not told what it is. But what possible use would heaven have for a 1970s-version super-computer, especially when we are told later about a "repository of knowledge":

> Then I realized that this was a library of the mind. By simply reflecting on a topic, as I had earlier in Christ's presence, all knowledge on that topic came to me. . . . No knowledge was kept from me, and it was impossible not to understand correctly every thought, every statement, every particle of knowledge.

page 76

The credibility of Eadie's story breaks down not only with such improbable narrative but, more significantly, in what it omits.

A Vacant Throne

One would expect—given the powerful descriptions in Revelation of God's dwelling place, where the four living creatures and the 24 elders never stop giving glory to the

One who sits on the throne—that a visit to heaven would ring with testimony to the glory of God. This visit does not. God is, in Betty Eadie's realm of the heavenlies, most conspicuous by His absence. We read of her meeting various spirit beings and "guardian angels," and we have already been informed that Jesus is a being separate from God, but at no point does she describe meeting God Himself.

Nor is a word spoken in Betty Eadie's heaven about the event that makes reconciliation with God possible: the sacrificial death on the cross of Jesus Christ, the Lamb slain from the foundation of the earth for the sins of mankind. Her Jesus has no nailprints in his hands, nor does he speak of salvation by faith, the resurrection, final judgment and other fundamental Christian doctrines.

In short, *Embraced by the Light* appears to be something other than a visit to heaven. In fact, the word *heaven* itself is never even used by Eadie to describe the place she visited. Why is this?

The answer might be found in the fact that Betty Eadie is a member of the Church of Jesus Christ of Latter-Day Saints, also known as the Mormons. According to Mormon teaching, the dead return to the spirit world where they continue to procreate and found new worlds throughout the universe. Eadie relates visits to such "glorious and perfect worlds" in other galaxies populated by "our spiritual brothers and sisters" (p. 88). This, then, may explain why the biblical term *heaven* is avoided: Quite another reality is being described.

Also, the Jesus encountered in *Embraced by the Light* is fully compatible with Eadie's own religion. In Mormon doctrine Jesus is not God in the triune sense but is called "our elder brother."[3] We ourselves can become as he is.

The omission of important biblical doctrines points to Eadie's link to Mormonism. And the fact should not be lost that Mormonism itself was begun by a vision of an "angel" in 1820 to fourteen-year-old Joseph Smith. Dick Baer, founder of Ex-Mormons and Christian Alliance, comments:

> This book is a carefully crafted book of deception . . . crafted to denigrate Christianity and promote doctrines that are mainline Mormon doctrines.[4]

One moving aspect of Betty Eadie's story occurs after she returns to her body, recovers from her illness and resumes her normal life. She tells a heart-rending account of how an infant foster child of theirs was later abused by her adoptive parents, after which Eadie and her husband were awarded custody. Reading of her love and concern for the child, one cannot help but hope that Betty Eadie will not continue to be deceived—and deceive others—with a counterfeit near-death experience. However sincere her account may seem, its objective evaluation reveals, in light of Scripture, glaring omissions and contradictions.

The question remains as to the nature of her experience. How exactly was she deceived and what were the spirit guides with whom she claims to have spoken? The apostle Paul, talking about highly visible teachers in the first-century Church, gives a salient warning about spiritual deception:

> Such men are false apostles, deceitful workmen, masquerading as apostles of Christ. And no wonder, *for Satan himself masquerades as an angel of light.* It is not surprising, then, if his servants masquerade as servants of righteousness. Their end will be what their actions deserve.
>
> 2 Corinthians 11:13–15 (italics mine)

Conclusion

We have seen in Betty Eadie's story yet another purported manifestation of spiritual forces. Here we see more
clearly the purpose of such "angels": to undermine ortho-
dox Christian teaching. Such religious "reeducation," as
we shall see, will eventually prepare the way for the coming of the Antichrist.

Grasping the fact that Satan and his servants have the
power to present themselves as benevolent supernatural
beings can mean a quantum leap for our understanding
of spiritual deception. On the pages that follow we will
utilize this axiom as we examine the multifarious and
extraordinary faces of spiritual deception. And we will
scrutinize the credentials of spiritual entities from other
metaphysical dimensions.

Betty Eadie's visit to the spiritual realm, though ultimately misleading, appears to have been for her a positive, uplifting experience. But such agreeable counterfeits
are overlaid with anti-Christian teachings that lead many
astray. And there is a dark side to the deception in which
men, women and children report horrific experiences of
being carried away in sheer terror by dreadful spirit
beings.

This, too, has its evil purpose, and it is to the forbid-
ding world of alien abductions that we now turn.

4

We Are Not Alone

The story begins innocently enough. Moderately successful writer retires with wife and young son to their secluded cabin in upstate New York for a quiet winter retreat away from the pressures of life in the Big Apple. But this would be no ordinary weekend. Author Whitley Strieber, along with countless readers of his bestselling books describing his fantastic experiences, would never be the same.

It was Christmas Day 1985. A thick blanket of freshly fallen snow provided an ideal opportunity for their son to break in his new sled. After cross-country skiing in the afternoon, the family returned to dinner of leftover Christmas goose, cranberry sauce and cold sweet potatoes. After their son went to bed, Strieber and his wife sat up reading quietly and listening to music. According to Strieber's account in his book *Communion,* he and his wife retired around ten o'clock and were fast asleep by eleven as the snow fell silently outside: an ordinary holiday evening in what appears to be an ordinary life.

But unknown to the sleeping family, another reality was poised to come crashing like a locomotive through the living room wall, thrusting Strieber into a world more macabre than anything in the horror novels he specialized in writing.

What follows is so incredible, so far beyond the pale of ordinary human experience, that some will dismiss the account as a feverish dream or outright lie. Before we continue with Strieber's story, then, let's pause to ask whether it lies within the realm of possibility that encounters with non-human entities could actually occur.

To a large extent the answer lies in another question: Do demonic forces actually exist and are they able to manifest their presence under certain limited circumstances? The Bible clearly says yes. Jesus Himself encountered the effects of spirit activity on numerous occasions, such as when He met the demon-possessed man at Capernaum (Mark 1:23–26), the Gerasene madman who dwelled in caves (Mark 5:1–17) and the woman disabled by an evil spirit for eighteen years (Luke 13:10–13). Another time He delivered a boy tormented by a demon that caused frightful convulsions (Mark 9:17–29).

The bizarre accounts of Strieber and others we will discuss have by no means been proven to the satisfaction of all, including me. But given the fact that the Bible is unequivocal about the reality of evil spirits from another dimension, we should remain open to the possibility that the extraordinary events we will be examining may actually have occurred.

Researchers into the occult are well aware of manifold ways by which demonic beings attempt first to seduce, then to corrupt and finally to terrorize and destroy souls. Thus are we commanded to "put on the full armor of God so that you can take your stand against the devil's schemes" (Ephesians 6:11). The Greek word translated

schemes in this passage has the meaning of "cunning stratagems." We must not forget we are dealing with ancient,
irremediably depraved spirits in possession of intelligence
and powers far eclipsing our own. At the same time, however, we should never lose sight of the wonderful assurance that those in Christ need not fear evil powers, for
"the one who is in you is greater than the one who is in
the world" (1 John 4:4).

Thus prepared, let us resume our macabre account.

Curiously, other than vague feelings of disquiet as if
after a forgotten nightmare, Strieber awoke the next
morning with little recollection of what would later
emerge as his astonishing ordeal of the previous night. In
the following days and weeks, however, Strieber's family
noticed a deterioration in his personality marked by
extreme mood changes, an inability to concentrate and
paranoid tendencies.

As he describes it, the despair of not understanding
what was happening to him led Strieber one day, as he
gazed out the window of his New York City high-rise
office, to contemplate suicide. At that point he sought
help from New York artist-turned-UFO-abduction-
researcher Budd Hopkins, author of *Missing Time* and
Intruders. Hopkins in turn referred Strieber to Dr. Donald Klein, who would guide him in hypnotic regression
to learn what had actually happened on that fateful
evening. Christmas night 1985, as it turns out, was only
one in a series of almost indescribable encounters stretching back into his childhood.

Whitley Strieber is (as we shall see) by no means unique.
His experience has been duplicated in hundreds, if not
thousands, of known cases over the past several years.

But we are getting ahead of our story. What did happen in the dead of night on that wintry evening in
Strieber's cabin in upstate New York? What follows is a

purportedly truthful account of an incredible episode that emerged as a result of hypnotic regression.

The Visitors

In the middle of Christmas night, Strieber writes, he suddenly found himself awake, not in a dreamlike half-sleep but alert and in full possession of his faculties. He could, as he puts it, have gotten up, read a book or gone for a walk in the snow; it was *that* kind of awake.

Nothing unusual in that; we have all experienced periods of wakefulness, for whatever reason, in the wee hours. Now comes the locomotive. In Strieber's own words:

> I heard a peculiar whooshing, swirling noise coming from the living room downstairs. This was no random creak, no settling of the house, but a sound *as if a large number of people were moving rapidly around in the room*.[1]
>
> page 11 (italics mine)

It is worth pointing out here (though we will reserve our analysis of Strieber's experience for later) that the abduction phenomenon typically involves the manipulation of each of the five senses. In this instance, the sound of commotion downstairs is heard only by Whitney Strieber, while his wife and son apparently remain asleep.

In any event, the nature of the phenomenon rapidly changes. But Strieber, although shocked and suddenly fearful for the safety of his family, does not react as one would expect:

> What I did next may seem peculiar. I settled back in bed. For some reason the extreme strangeness of what I was hearing did not rouse me to action. Over the course of this narrative this sort of inappropriate response will be repeated many times. If something is strange enough, the response is very

different from what one would think. The mind seems to
tune out as if by some sort of instinct.

page 11

The inconceivable episode, however, had just begun. No
sooner had he settled back when he noticed that the bedroom door, which had been open, was closing slowly. Someone or something was moving it. Instantly alarmed, Strieber
sat up again in bed next to his wife, his heart pounding.
Could it be their son coming to their room—or a midnight
prowler? This latter possibility, unnerving as it might have
been, was shattered by what happened next:

> Then I saw edging around it a compact figure. It was so dis-
> tinct and yet so completely, impossibly astonishing that at
> first I could not understand it at all. I simply sat there star-
> ing, too stunned to move.

page 12

Strieber then describes this "entity" (for lack of a better term) as about three and a half feet tall and smaller
and lighter than his son. It was dressed in odd, costume-
like apparel, with a nondescript face consisting of "two
dark holes for eyes and a black, downturned line of a
mouth that later became an O" (p. 12).

Strieber's mind, understandably, had difficulty taking
in this assault on his visual senses. He believed he was
wide-awake and alert, but this was so impossible there
had to be another explanation. Could it be a dreamlike
illusion that occurs sometimes between waking and sleep?
His wife lay sound asleep beside him as if in a trancelike
state (as she did during all Strieber's nocturnal confrontations), oblivious to what was happening.

The next thing Strieber remembers is the figure rush-
ing toward him, followed by blackness as he apparently
loses consciousness.

Now comes the first of many shiftings of location that seem common to these experiences. He finds himself transported to what he describes as a "small sort of depression" in the woods. As he sits on the frozen earth, he is startled by the absence of snow on the ground. It is winter; where is the snow? There is no use resisting. Strieber is powerless to put up any kind of struggle against the forces acting upon him:

> I felt that I was under the exact and detailed control of whomever had me. I could not move my head, or my hands, or any part of my body save for my eyes. Despite this, I was not tied.
>
> page 15

Then Strieber notices he is not alone in the wooded depression. Other entities are around him, one of whom is "working busily at something that seemed to have to do with the right side of my head. It wore dark-blue coveralls and was extremely fast" (p. 15). This activity in connection with Strieber's head seems related to a later "operation" that he undergoes at the hands of his abductors. Such operations are one of the most ominous features of abduction cases, leading to speculation that human consciousness is being altered in some unfathomable way.

Strieber is then transported above the forest into the black night sky, where he finds himself "sitting in a messy round room" apparently in the bowels of an alien spacecraft. This is no detached, dreamlike experience: Strieber repeatedly describes his emotional state in the most graphic of terms:

> While I had up until that point been able to retain a degree of control of [sic] my attention, this now left me and I became entirely given over to extreme dread. The fear was so pow-

erful that it seemed to make my personality completely evaporate. This was not a theoretical or even a mental experience, but something profoundly physical. "Whitley" ceased to exist. What was left was a body in a state of raw fear so great that it swept about me like a thick, suffocating curtain, turning paralysis into a condition that seemed close to death. I do not think that my ordinary humanity survived the transition to this little room. I died, and a wild animal appeared in my place.

page 16

Set all skepticism aside for a moment and imagine your own reaction to such a thing happening to you. How would *you* react? Under the circumstances, Strieber's reaction appears understandable, even normal.

He mentions peculiar details of the room in which he found himself. It gave him the impression of an unkempt, even dirty living space with clothing strewn on the floor. Several other varieties of entities were also in the room:

I was aware that I had seen four different types of figures. The first was the small robotlike being that had led the way into my bedroom. He was followed by a large group of short, stocky ones in the dark blue coveralls.

These had wide faces, appearing either dark gray or dark blue in that light, with glittering deep-set eyes, pug noses, and broad, somewhat human mouths. Inside the room, I encountered two types of creatures that did not look at all human. The most provocative of these was about five feet tall, very slender and delicate, with extremely prominent and mesmerizing black slanted eyes. This being had an almost vestigial mouth and nose. The huddled figures in the theater were somewhat smaller, with similarly shaped heads but round, black eyes like large buttons.[2]

page 20

Strieber is shown a shiny needle and informed that it is to be inserted into his brain. On hearing this he becomes "quite simply crazed with terror" and attempts to argue with his captors, to no avail. Physical resistance proves impossible; it is as if he no longer controls his body. Suddenly there is a bang and a flash, and Strieber realizes to his horror that some kind of "operation" has been performed on his brain.

As if this were not terrifying enough, worse is yet to come:

> The next thing I knew I was being shown an enormous and extremely ugly object, gray and scaly, with a sort of network of wires on the end. It was at least a foot long, narrow, and triangular in structure. They inserted this thing into my rectum. It seemed to swarm into me as if it had a life of its own. Apparently its purpose was to take samples, possibly of fecal matter, but at the time I had the impression that I was being raped, and for the first time I felt anger.
>
> page 21

This kind of involuntary and forced examination is, as we shall see, a prominent feature of abduction accounts. In Strieber's case, the last thing he recalls is a small incision made on his right hand by one of the entities as if to draw blood. Then his memories end abruptly, and the next thing he knows it is morning.

It may be that he blocked the experience subconsciously because it was so unimaginably horrible. For whatever reason, Strieber had no distinct memories at first of what had happened to him. But after his nighttime abduction he began to suffer inexplicable physical discomforts. He reports suffering rectal pain and having trouble sitting. At the same time he complained of pain behind his right ear, where an unexplainable pinprick scar could be seen. His right forefinger became infected as if from a splinter.

Prying the Lid Off Pandora's Box

In Whitley Strieber's increasingly complicated saga, the bizarre events tumble one after the other until it is impossible to discern reality from science fiction. Reading it is like stumbling into a B-grade horror movie. Is Strieber making it all up? Things like this could not possibly be true! Or could they? Strieber insists he is telling the truth and buttresses his claim with affidavits from psychiatrists and polygraph test results.

Whatever the reality of Strieber's own account, a growing body of evidence indicates that something bizarre is indeed going on. Later on we will see, moreover, that there is a sound biblical explanation for such phenomena.

Through hypnotic regression under the supervision of his psychiatrist, Dr. Donald Klein, other episodes came to light. Strieber had troubling, confused memories about another recent evening. It now appeared that the night of October 4 in upper New York State held another abduction experience. Excerpts from the transcripts of Strieber's regression paint a picture of inexpressible terror as an entity entered his bedroom that night and came toward him:

> I saw something that looked like it had a hood on it, standing over by the wall near the corner in our bedroom [breaks into panic] and I don't want it to be there! I don't want it to be there! Please! God, it—What's it doing to me? Stop! Oh, oh, stop! What's it doing to me? [Screams, prolonged, twenty seconds.] (I cannot recall experiencing at any time in my life such panic as was evoked at this point in hypnosis. . . . I then emerged spontaneously from hypnosis. No written words, nothing, can convey my feelings at that moment. All I can say is that I relived fear so raw, profound, and large that I would not have thought it possible that such an emotion could exist.)[3]

page 54

According to the transcripts of this session, again under the supervision of Dr. Klein, Strieber recounts how the being touches his head with something resembling a magic wand. His head immediately explodes with a vision of planet earth engulfed in flames and other dark, ominous scenes. Nothing more of significance appears to transpire that night.

Three weeks later Strieber's bedroom is invaded by a horde of short creatures dressed again in what look like blue coveralls. He is spirited out of the room and finds himself in a strange, undersized round room that, in his own words, "smells kind of nasty. . . . It's not clean in here" (p. 75). An operation, similar to the one described earlier, is performed while his abductors take an unusual interest in Strieber's sexual responses. Then one of the beings makes a dramatic pronouncement: "You are our chosen one" (p. 76).

Strieber reacts with incredulity at what he suspects is a cynical attempt to manipulate him. Shortly afterward he "sails back" through the night skies, landing in the living room of his cabin. Returning upstairs and crawling into bed, a shocked and exhausted Strieber longs to "live in a prison" where he would presumably be safe from such bizarre nocturnal abductions.

Given the increasingly bizarre experiences described in *Communion* and its sequel, *Transformation*, one wonders why Strieber ever dared set foot in his cabin!

Whatever the reason for Strieber's persistent alien encounters, one thing is clear: He has reaped enormous profits from his experiences. Upon its release in 1987, *Communion* jumped to the top of the *New York Times* bestseller list, where it stayed for almost a year.

There appears to be a deep and growing fascination with UFOs and especially abduction experiences. And it is a matter of more than academic interest: Researchers estimate the number of UFO sightings worldwide to be in the millions. As for "close encounters" like those experienced by Whitley Strieber, there are currently between five and ten thousand documented cases.[4]

Won't You Be My Neighbor?

Given that *something* is happening, the next question is, How do we explain it? Most UFO research groups in the United States cling stubbornly to what is called the Extraterrestrial Hypothesis (ETH), despite the fact that this hypothesis has been abandoned by investigators in Europe and the rest of the world.[5] According to the ETH, all genuine UFO phenomena, including "close encounters" and abductions, are caused by space travelers from other inhabited planets who have traveled to earth. This view is so pervasive among the American public that many are blithely unaware of any other explanation, barring total skepticism.

There *is* another explanation. But for now we must ask what evidence exists that interplanetary creatures from outer space are invading our atmosphere. The answer, surprisingly, is that it is highly *un*likely. Let's take a look at some of the problems with the ETH.

Long Ago and Far Away

The average citizen has little conception of the vast distances involved in space travel. According to modern physics, it is impossible for a physical object to exceed the speed of light, which is 186,000 miles per second. By comparison, the NASA space shuttle crawls along at a mere 24,000 miles per *hour*. Even the speed of light, however, is not fast enough to get around the universe in any meaningful length of time.

The reason, according to astronomers, is that the regions of space thought most likely to support highly evolved life forms are millions of light-years away from earth. In order to appreciate the fantastic distances one would have to travel, we need to keep in mind that a light-year is the distance light travels in one year—*at a speed of 186,000 miles per second.*

Let's stop and think about the ramifications of this astounding distance. Suppose, for instance, that an interplanetary spacecraft decided to pay planet earth a social call. What would such a trip entail?

First, it would mean leaving for earth long before *Homo sapiens* (according to evolutionary theory) even appeared on the planet. In order to arrive in our atmosphere *now,* an interplanetary vehicle would have had to begin its journey literally millions of years ago. How odd, then, that we have so many reports of aliens emerging from UFOs claiming to be delivering a message to mankind, when humankind did not even exist when they began their journey (and totally apart from the likelihood of space visitors being able to survive a one-way trip of millions of years!).

These "messages" are in themselves very revealing. We will discuss them later. For now, it is important to note another fact: While these aliens are supposedly coming to deliver a message to mankind—for example, about the ecological dangers to our planet or the nuclear threat—their own civilizations and planet will doubtless have passed out of existence. Why would this be the case? Remember, we are talking about *millions of years* of space travel just to get here, not counting the return trip. What happens to a civilization in a million years? We do not have any answers to that question, except to note that exceedingly few human civilizations have managed to struggle on for even a millennium or longer.

So we have the unlikely prospect of aliens concerned about the destruction of earthly rain forests when their own planet has in all likelihood turned into a charred cinder; and the unlikely prospect of aliens taking an interest in our insignificant planet when some scientists estimate there are ten thousand civilizations *in our own galaxy alone.* Before the overload buzzer starts beeping in our brains, let me get in one more fact: Astronomers believe there are more than *five hundred billion* galaxies in the known universe. Multiply five hundred billion by ten thousand, and you will arrive at a rough estimate of the number of planetary civilizations thought to exist.

For the sake of argument, let's suppose there is indeed such an incalculable number of inhabited planets out there, all presumably in various evolutionary stages of growing, developing and dying. Is it not puzzling that alien creatures should offer cryptic warnings about ecological disaster to their chosen abductees in the dead of night under highly questionable circumstances?

And why us? What is so unusual—or threatening—about what is happening on earth that sets us apart in an intergalactic sea of inhabited planets? Peter Hough, taking note of the tremendous diversity to be found among reports of UFOs and aliens, remarks:

> These hundreds of conflicting descriptions weigh heavily against the supposition that many UFOs are spacecraft piloted by extraterrestrial visitors. For this would imply that Earth is some sort of Galactic Mecca for hundreds of different space travelling civilizations. Yet it is the occupants themselves who encourage this unlikely myth, with alleged messages on the lines of: "We are aliens from planet X, friendly and concerned for the well being of your world. Stop tinkering with nuclear energy before it is too late. . . ."[6]

The reader is correct in thinking it makes *no* sense that we would be so popular. But it gets even more unbelievable. Take, for instance, the apparent fact that UFOs come in a wide variety of shapes and colors and range in size from that of a flying refrigerator to enormous crafts hundreds of meters across. Predictably, the same is true of UFO occupants. Another British researcher, John Rimmer, continues to shred the Extraterrestrial Hypothesis:

> Can the ETH explain why there seem to be so many *different* kinds of creatures? Although there are broad similarities in many cases, nearly all are different to some significant degree: short, big-headed creatures; human figures; monkey-like aliens; one-eyed monsters; creatures with one leg; creatures with webbed fingers; some speak fluent English, others communicate with grunts and signs, others seem to be telepathic; all this without mentioning the equally varied forms of craft involved. If we take all the accounts at face value it would seem that almost every abduction has been the work of a separate race of alien visitors.[7]

The fact that virtually all aliens appear to breathe and move about adequately in our atmosphere raises another red flag. This would not be possible unless they came from a planet with the same atmospheric composition and gravitational pull as that of earth. Recall the televised pictures of the Apollo astronauts leaping about with abandon on the surface of the moon. With no atmosphere and only a third of the gravitational pull of earth, the moon caused a noticeable change in how the "aliens" (in this case, the NASA astronauts) got around. So is it not strange that the UFO aliens apparently encounter no problems breathing or walking? What are the chances that the aliens' own planets would have a similar atmosphere and gravitational pull to ours? Even a small change from earth's parameters would be immediately noticeable.[8]

Practicing Medicine without a License

One of the most appalling features of abduction reports is what are described as the "examinations" that frequently inflict considerable pain and discomfort on the abductee. Dr. Richard Neal, Jr., M.D., a specialist in the physical effects of abductions, has investigated the physical trauma associated with close encounters with UFOs. These include merciless intrusions into the abductee's body, which often leave permanent scars:

> The nasal cavity, ears, eyes and genitalia appear to be the physical areas of greatest interest to abducting aliens. The umbilical region (navel) is as well, but in females only. Many abductees have described a thin probe with a tiny ball on its end being inserted into the nostril—usually on the right side. They are able to hear a "crushing" type of sound as the bone in this area is apparently being penetrated. Many will have nosebleeds following these examinations.[9]

This is precisely what Whitley Strieber describes as having happened during one of his abductions, the only difference being that the intrusion was into his left nostril:

> I had the distinct impression that there was something in my left nostril, and that it was being slowly moved far up my nose. When I tried to struggle, I heard a pop like an apple crunching between my eyes.[10]

page 124

Some abductees report being forced to do things that serve no conceivable purpose other than to humiliate and traumatize them. Strieber recounts having to eat some kind of fruit with the taste and consistency of a rotten pomegranate. During another abduction he was forced to swallow a milky substance that left a "horrid taste" in his mouth.[11]

Moving from the crude to the grotesque, we discover that this is only the beginning of indignities forced on abductees. Veteran UFO investigator Raymond Fowler has followed the strange case of Betty Andreasson since her initial abduction in 1967. In his book *The Watchers: The Secret Design Behind UFO Abduction*, Fowler describes Andreasson's hypnotic recall of a bizarre operation aboard an alien spaceship. (We will look at her experiences in detail in chapter 13.) Andreasson believes she was abducted in order to comfort another abductee lying on a table:

> Betty continued to describe forgotten memories that unfolded before her. An alien brings her down to where other aliens are working near the woman's legs. Betty is shocked to the core to see them removing a very small, strange-looking *fetus!* What they then do to the infant horrifies her.[12]

Needles are attached to the head of the fetus and its eyelids are circumcised. It is then put into some kind of glass container filled with liquid to which are connected something like electrodes.

Here we have one of many reported accounts of aliens impregnating human women in order to remove the fetuses later for some inconceivable purpose. Fowler theorizes that Betty witnessed "a product of genetic engineering," and that the removed fetus "was one of many bred by *The Watchers* as part of their genetics program."[13]

This frankly unbelievable reason for alien abductions is echoed by researcher Budd Hopkins, who first investigated the Whitley Strieber case. After examining numerous case histories of female abductions in his book *Intruders,* Hopkins concludes:

> A central goal of UFO abduction, I now believe, is the apparent interbreeding of an alien species with our own. And that process, it would seem, is both covert and very widespread.[14]

This interplanetary inbreeding allegedly does not end with the conception of the half-human, half-alien creature. According to Hopkins, the "parents" are often shown their space children at a later date:

> Most bizarre of all, the humans—male or female—who have involuntarily provided cells are later abducted yet again and shown the results—tiny hybrid infants or children. In fact, they are asked to pick up and hold their "offspring" in a kind of bonding experience![15]

Medieval Butchers

Here we find a serious contradiction in the belief that aliens from highly advanced civilizations elsewhere in the universe have come to experiment on humans. If, as Fowler suggests, the aliens "could easily be a billion years or more ahead of man in evolutionary development,"[16] why are they conducting medical experiments with all the finesse of a backyard butcher?

Astrophysicist Jacques Vallee, one of the most astute and discerning researchers of UFO phenomena, turns his big guns on the notion of alien medical experimentation:

> The reported interaction with the occupants of the objects is absurd and their overtly "scientific" experiments are crude to the point of being grotesque. The "medical examination" to which abductees are said to be subjected, often accompanied by sadistic sexual manipulation, is reminiscent of the medieval tales of encounters with demons.[17]

And why the necessity of so many abductions allegedly to collect tissue and cells and perform examinations? Commenting on the large numbers of reported human guinea pigs, Vallee concludes:

The aliens would have to be very poor scientists indeed if they needed that many interventions to collect the kind of material any skilled human nurse could collect in a few hours, and without inducing trauma. What is in question here is the very idea that UFOs are extraterrestrial in the usual understanding of the term.[18]

Are They Publicity Shy?

One wonders why the alleged UFO aliens do not settle the question of their origin once and for all with an ET media event like a televised landing on the South Lawn of the White House. Here is where most enthusiasts of the Extraterrestrial Hypothesis avert their gaze, shuffle their feet and come up with ingenuous replies. Raymond Fowler insists that "official contact and release of their message by world leaders would cause chaos."[19]

But it is difficult to see the wisdom of the present *modus operandi*. One would think a vastly superior civilization with a critically important message for planet earth would take a more direct route than snatching people away in the dead of night and inflicting terrifying experiences on them.

Conclusion

Again, it is clear that something is going on quite different from the premise of this implausible hypothesis. Already in the mid–1970s, the most authoritative name in UFO investigative circles, the late Professor J. Allen Hynek of Northwestern University, had concluded that the ETH was untenable. Hynek, the scientific consultant for the official U.S. Air Force UFO investigation known as "Project Blue Book," stated:

I have come to support less and less the idea that UFOs are "nuts and bolts" spacecraft from other worlds. . . . There are just too many things going against this theory. To me, it seems ridiculous that super intelligence would travel great distances to do *relatively stupid things* like stop cars, collect soil samples, and frighten people. I think we must begin to reexamine the evidence. We must begin to look closer to home.[20]

Could it be that we are not insulated after all by vast expanses of deep space from what to all appearances are malevolent, predatory creatures? Is it possible that the evil one will use such entities to prepare the world for the coming of Antichrist? As with the "angelic hitchikers" and Betty Eadie's "angels," we shall presently see that UFO aliens also have a message for mankind. To understand this better we will now focus our discussion on the origin and nature of the UFO phenomena.

5

The Universe
Next Door

*Are We Looking in
the Wrong Dimension?*

The first thing apparent to most serious researchers is that, in the words of Professor Hynek, UFOs are not "nuts-and-bolts" physical constructions. The phenomenon is too capricious. Numerous reports exist of UFOs being picked up on radar screens, while on other occasions they are invisible to radar. They are observed executing what to current technology are impossible feats such as sharp turns at fantastic speeds. They change shape and color. They appear suddenly to astonished observers only to disappear into thin air.

Perhaps the most important indication of the non-physical nature of UFOs is the fact that despite literally hundreds of thousands of reports worldwide over the past few decades, few clear photographs of UFOs exist.

A Picture Is Worth a Thousand Words

Dr. Allen Tough summarizes the extant photographic evidence:

> A UFO has never been clearly photographed by two persons independently. There are extremely few *close-up* photos of an alien craft, and I do not know of one that has passed rigorous laboratory scrutiny of the negative. Angelo has pointed out that we lack irrefutable *physical* evidence of alien visitors and space ships; we have only "soft" human testimony (eye-witness reports) rather than "hard" technical and scientific data.[1]

This is an astounding admission. Despite the difficulties of photographing, especially at night, and the fact that most people do not carry cameras around with them, it is still striking that we do not have more first-class photographic evidence of this phenomenon. This is especially true when we consider that numerous sightings have been made in populated areas and viewed by multiple observers for significant lengths of time. In such cases it seems reasonable to expect that at least someone would run for a camera and take a series of good, clear photographs. As for the aliens themselves, the situation is even more inexplicable. Dr. Tough states bluntly that "there are no photographs of UFO occupants."[2]

With the growing number of abductee reports, we must ask ourselves why not a single clear shot of the aliens exists. It is possible to come away with the impression that whatever is out there is "teasing" humanity, giving the appearance of being a material, physical phenomenon—and all the time remaining just out of reach.

In his book *The Alien Agenda,* Dr. Clifford Wilson discusses numerous curious reports of UFO occupants making repairs to their apparently disabled spacecrafts. There are also reports of seemingly damaged parts dropping off UFOs, to which Wilson replies:

> If these beings do indeed come from outer space, and if there are the tens of thousands of UFOs that would be necessary to account for the worldwide sightings, obviously they would be supermachines, not regularly breaking down in such unlikely spots—just where they were sure to be seen by earthlings. It seems there is a deliberate attempt to make sure that their totally material nature is really believed in. Why? Is it, as John Keel suggests, "a cosmic hoax"?[3]

It is indeed difficult to imagine a spacecraft incomprehensibly technologically advanced navigating deep space, only to drop the cosmic equivalent of a muffler while tooling around in the atmosphere of earth. Such inexplicable behavior amounts to yet another nail in the coffin of the theory that UFOs are space travelers from other planets. The signs, in the words of Jacques Vallee, point to another explanation:

> In the final analysis the labyrinth of our expectations may be empty, and it may require a completely different approach to solve the problem of detecting and communicating with the *other forms of consciousness that probably fill the universe.*[4]

What might these "other forms of consciousness" be, and what do they want?

The Occult Connection

A thread can be traced through many of the abduction reports, a common denominator that keeps popping up.

But it is routinely ignored by UFO investigators who have no interest in anything that would lend support to what they consider a primitive, obsolete worldview.

Nevertheless, there exists a startling connection between UFOs and poltergeist activity—strange effects that in tradition and folklore have been attributed to ghosts and the spirits of the departed. Christians consider such activity to be the work of demonic spirits. How curious, then, to learn that many of those involved in UFO close encounters are dogged by paranormal experiences!

Whitley Strieber, for example, provides us with a virtual catalog of poltergeist activity. Note the following paranormal incidents found in his books.

Electronic Disturbances

In 1977 Strieber and his wife were sitting in their living room when suddenly a voice started speaking to them through their stereo, which had just finished playing a record. Addressing the voice, they were astonished when the voice answered back, conversing with them briefly. While ham radios, taxis and police radios can under rare conditions interrupt stereo equipment, it is quite impossible to hold a two-way conversation.

On other occasions Strieber's radio and television were inexplicably switched on and off, apparently at will.[5]

Physical Disturbances

During 1986, at the height of his abduction experiences, Strieber's cabin in upstate New York became a virtual haunted house:

> When night fell in the country the woods seemed to rise up around the house and clutch it with avid fingers. There was often a powerful feeling of presence. People would hear footsteps on our decks and porch, see lights shining in the win-

dows, hear strange whistling noises in the sky above the cabin.[6]

page 124

The most dramatic incident of this kind took place on the night of August 27, 1986, and occurred in conjunction with another alien visitation. Strieber was reading alone in the living room of his cabin late at night when suddenly "there came a knocking on the side of the house. This was a substantial noise, very regular and sharp" (p. 130).

It seemed as if a machine were pounding on the outside wall at a spot nearly twenty feet above the driveway. Strieber says he would have heard anyone attempting to move a ladder across the gravel, not to mention that the motion-sensitive burglar alarm would have been set off.

Animal Responses

Rappings on the walls of haunted houses are a well-known poltergeist activity. Another noteworthy aspect of Strieber's knocking incident, however, was the reaction of his two cats. "Both cats," according to Strieber, "were riveted with terror" (p. 130). The two cats fled, one of them to a bathroom linen shelf where it hid for nearly a full day before coming out.

Curious, Strieber tried to duplicate the knockings by propping a tall ladder against the house and pounding hard on the wall. Although he knocked as hard as the knockings he had heard, the cats remained indifferent.

It is well known among researchers of the paranormal that animals often serve as a barometer of occult activity. Dogs and cats, for instance, will often flee a place where "ghosts" or other occultic activities are present. Animals apparently have the ability to perceive spiritual forces that remain indiscernible to humans.[7]

Psychic Abilities

Strieber reveals in his books that he began to experience ever-deepening levels of psychic phenomena such as levitation and out-of-body-experiences (OBEs) during the night. After one such occasion, the next morning he became a channel for a disembodied spirit:

> When I told Anne about [the OBE], I found that it had yet another dimension. We discovered that when she asked me questions, I would hear a voice, very distinct, beside my right ear, which would give answers.
>
> pages 77–78

The initial dialogue between Strieber's wife and the entity speaking through Strieber is strikingly similar to that of spirit voices channeled through mediums:

> *Anne:* "Why did you come here?"
> *Voice:* "We saw a glow."
> *Anne:* "Why are you doing this to Whitley?"
> *Voice:* "It is time."
> *Anne:* "Where are you from?"
> *Voice:* "Everywhere."
> *Anne:* "What is the earth?"
> *Voice:* "It is a school."
>
> page 79

At this point the voice changed, no longer a distinct audible sound but, according to Strieber, "more thought-like." Of special interest is the fact that the answers given by the entity reflect Eastern, occultic philosophy.[8] This, as we shall later see, is a central aspect of alien messages to mankind.

Another characteristic of spirit channeling is evident here: the cryptic nature of the responses, which usually offer little concrete information and raise more questions than they answer. In the Colyn Smythe spirit recordings, which elicited considerable interest in England in the early 1970s, the same staccato, abrupt responses were recorded, as one observer noted: "Unfortunately the answers were short and rarely very informative. Repeatedly, the voices appeared to avoid direct questions and insisted on being taken at 'face value.'"[9]

Such spirit communication also betrays a noticeable arrogance and ambivalence toward the inquirer, giving the distinct impression that the spirits have no intention of being particularly helpful. The Bible speaks of "deceiving spirits" that are demons (1 Timothy 4:1) and that evidently have the ability to use or mimic human voices.

Whitley Strieber is but one of countless examples of the connection between occult activity and UFO abductee experiences. A report from the British UFO Research Association (BUFORA) states that "witnesses who claim psychic experiences tend to be more likely to have a CE 4 [abduction]. Even those who have not had any psychic experiences (PSI) often find these stimulated by the close encounter."[10] This fact should in itself offer sufficient warning that we are dealing not with another planet, but with demonic forces from a parallel dimension.

They Love Darkness Rather Than Light

There is yet another telling aspect of the UFO abduction phenomenon: Not only angelic hitchhikers are encountered along roads on dark nights. The BUFORA report notes that "a great number of abduction cases seem to begin with the abductee driving along a lonely road late at night."[11]

This is exactly the setting for the first publicized abduction and perhaps the most famous of all: the case of Betty and Barney Hill, whose experience is related in the book *The Interrupted Journey*.[12]

Barney Hill himself had been a resolute skeptic regarding the possibility of UFOs. But while driving through the White Mountains in New Hampshire on their way home from Canada during the night of September 19, 1961, with their dog in the back seat, the Hills found themselves being trailed by what appeared to be a bright star. For the first hour or so they took little notice of it, assuming it was perhaps an orbiting satellite. As the night deepened, however, and they drove on through the remote region with the road virtually to themselves, the light in the sky grew brighter. More ominously, it seemed to be following their automobile.

The Hills' anxiety increased as the object drew closer. Finally it drew close enough that through binoculars they could see it was some kind of craft. Could it be an airplane or helicopter? But the object made no sound as it trailed them just out of view over the treeline. Whatever it was, it was playing cat and mouse with Betty and Barney, matching their speed as they slowed to try to get a better look at it. Try as they might, they could catch only glimpses of it through the trees.

They were on the verge of panic, being stalked by a mammoth-sized craft gliding silently overhead. Finally Barney slowed to a stop in the middle of the deserted road to try to determine once and for all what it was. The only sound in the eerily quiet night was the purr of the motor of their own car. Every fiber of Barney's being (as he said later) rebelled against what his eyes were seeing. Grabbing the binoculars, he opened the car door and stepped out onto the warm pavement:

> As he did so, the huge object—as wide in diameter as the distance between three telephone poles along the road, Barney later described it—swung in a silent arc directly across the road, not more than a hundred feet from him. The double row of windows was now clear and obvious.

> page 30

An awestruck Hill found himself inexplicably propelled across the road to a field where the UFO was now hovering at tree level. Drawn closer against his will, he looked through his binoculars to see strange-looking figures peering out at him through the portholes of the craft. He was seized with the alarming impression that something evil was about to happen:

> As the focus became sharp, he remembers the eyes of the one crew member who stared down at him. Barney had never seen eyes like that before. With all his energy he ripped the binoculars from his eyes and ran screaming back across the field to Betty and the car. . . . Barney was near hysteria. He jammed the car into first gear, spurting off down the road, shouting that he was sure they were going to be captured.
>
> page 32

The Hills drove down the road in stark panic, craning their necks to see if they were being followed. Suddenly they heard a strange noise:

> The car seemed to vibrate with it. It was in irregular rhythm— beep, beep—beep, beep, beep, beep—seeming to come from behind the car, in the direction of the trunk. Barney said, "What's that noise?" Betty said, "I don't know." They each began to feel an odd tingling drowsiness come over them. From that moment, a sort of haze came over them.
>
> page 33

Some time later the beeping noise began again and the Hills found themselves driving down the road, but in a different vicinity. When they arrived home in a state of shock, they discovered that the trip had taken longer than it should have. Somehow an inexplicable loss of time had occurred.

What follows is the paradigm case of alien abduction. At first the Hills exhibited signs of traumatic amnesia, which is the body's natural defense mechanism to repress an experience of stark terror, as Budd Hopkins writes:

> One of the central ideas in *Missing Time* was my guess that many people—perhaps thousands—may have had UFO abduction experiences and yet *consciously* remember almost nothing to indicate they had suffered these traumatic encounters. The pattern of evidence we had uncovered suggests that a kind of "enforced" amnesia can efficiently erase from conscious memory all but the very slightest recollections of such experiences.[13]

Gradually the Hills began to recall bits and pieces of an extraordinary, unearthly experience aboard an alien spacecraft. Evidently their minds had been suppressing the indescribable ordeal. All the classic features were present that have become familiar to abduction researchers: a bizarre, terrifying examination at the hands of short, almond-eyed creatures, followed by frightful physical aftereffects. Even their dog had been whining and cowering in the back seat.

Let's step back for a moment to take an objective look at the Betty and Barney Hill incident. At first glance it appears to vindicate the ETH—the theory that alien-manned space vehicles, presumably from distant, highly advanced planets, are present in our atmosphere.

But what possible reason would interstellar entities have in terrorizing people driving down a lonely road, playing cat and mouse with them before allegedly subjecting them to crude and unmentionable indignities? And back to our earlier question: Why does it happen so often under cover of darkness?

Jacques Vallee has done a statistical analysis of UFO sightings and encounters worldwide. The results show a typical bell curve, with the majority of incidents occurring in the dead of night:

On these curves it can be seen that the number of close encounters is very low during the daylight hours. It starts increasing about five P.M. and reaches a maximum about nine P.M. It then decreases steadily until one A.M., then rises again to a secondary peak about three A.M. and returns to its low diurnal level by six [A.M.].[14]

These results, confirmed by other researchers, demonstrate that the aliens prefer to operate under cover of darkness. This should remind us of occultism, the practices of which traditionally take place at night and usually in obscure settings. In the New Testament Jesus explains why:

> This is the verdict: Light has come into the world, but men loved darkness instead of light because their deeds were evil. Everyone who does evil hates the light, and will not come into the light for fear that his deeds will be exposed.
>
> John 3:19–20

No convincing explanation exists for the demonstrable predilection of UFOs and aliens for darkness other than the explanation that *it suits their nature.*

The evidence thus far indicates that the UFO phenomenon is the work of non-material entities that hate and fear the light of day.

Robert Fowler is one of a growing number of abduction researchers admitting this spiritual aspect. He describes how his own views were "slowly but surely honed to accommodate ever deeper levels of the psychic component found in the UFO experience."[15]

A Parallel, Hostile Dimension

The closer we examine the occult connection, the stronger we find the link. UFO investigator John Keel notes:

A person who has a long history of prophetic dreams and other psychic experiences might be known to the local gossips as a crackpot and would rate low on the reliability scale. But extensive UFO studies have shown that this is also the kind of person *most likely* to have a genuine low-level or landing sighting. Their psychic ability might also make them susceptible to receiving a telepathic message or undergoing something even stranger.[16]

We turn again to the case of Whitley Strieber, who makes a startling admission:

> For half of my life I have been engaged in a rigorous and detailed search for a finer state of consciousness. Now I thought my mind was turning against me, that my years of eager study of everything from Zen to quantum physics had led me into some strange and tragic byway of the soul.[17]

This statement, offered by Strieber almost as an afterthought, conveys a truth more significant than he intended. His "rigorous and detailed search" included many years of involvement with the mystical philosophy of the Gurdjieff Foundation, as well as meditation practices. In an interview with author Douglas Winter, Strieber claimed: "I have been a witch. I have experimented with worshiping the earth as a goddess/mother."[18]

Although most researchers deride the possibility that UFOs and close encounters with aliens are occultic phenomena, the connection is unmistakable. Lynn Catoe, bibliographer for the Library of Congress, concluded in reviewing some 1,600 books and articles on the subject that many UFO reports "recount alleged incidents that are strikingly familiar to demonic possession and psychic phenomena which have long been known to theologians and parapsychologists."[19]

The possibility that the UFO phenomenon is caused by occultic spiritual forces puts the matter in a new light. Instead of being space travelers from distant galaxies, the entities actually come from another parallel dimension. They are described in the Bible as unrelentingly hostile to the human race in general and to believers in particular:

> Our struggle is not against flesh and blood, but against the rulers, against the authorities, against the powers of this dark world and against the spiritual forces of evil in the heavenly realms.
>
> Ephesians 6:12

The experiences of Whitley Strieber, the Hills and countless others amply demonstrate that contacts with UFOs and aliens are negative in the extreme. In fact, as noted in the BUFORA report, studies indicate that "fear is the most common reaction" to close encounters with UFOs.[20]

UFO investigators who reject the biblical view of the supernatural world explain the negative reactions of abductees as merely the "fear of the unknown." The terror that abductees, even animals, feel, however, cannot be explained away so easily. If the aliens were really good and wise beyond our imagination, surely they would be able to relate to humans in a more positive way. Strieber, who steadfastly refuses to admit the evil nature of his abductors, nevertheless admits "[m]ostly, they terrified me. One does not want to develop a relationship with a hungry panther."[21]

Extraterrestrial Evangelists

Happily we are not left in perpetual limbo regarding the nature of UFOs and their alien occupants. Those who take the Bible seriously are provided with the means for checking the credentials of the space creatures. The apostle Paul gives an important principle when dealing with spiritual phenomena:

> Even if we or an angel from heaven should preach a gospel other than the one we preached to you, let him be eternally condemned! As we have already said, so now I say again: If anybody is preaching to you a gospel other than what you accepted, let him be eternally condemned!
>
> Galatians 1:8–9

These strong words indicate that spiritual deception is an ever-present danger. One must examine the teachings, or "message," to know whether it is in agreement with God's truth as revealed in the Bible. In the case of UFO aliens, this is relatively easy since they have been forthright in dictating their garbled versions of ultimate truth to planet earth.

The only problem is *which* alien "gospel" to examine, since there are multitudes of messages passed along to abductees. A common theme is the ecological-apocalyptic warning: *Watch out or you'll ruin things for the whole galaxy.*

A plea for environmental responsibility would not in itself be cause for alarm. But that is usually not the primary impact of their message. Rather, contact with aliens seems to have a profound effect on the spiritual outlook of abductees. This is shown by what happened to Whitley Strieber's son while the Striebers were staying at their cabin.

On the night of April 2, 1986, Whitley awoke in the middle of the night and went down to check on his son. He was appalled to discover him missing. A frantic search of the house failed to turn him up. While checking outside he noticed a huge black object in the sky above. Then he heard an audible voice say, "Can you go back upstairs by yourself or do you want us to help you?" Just then he saw the dark forms of three aliens looming above the bushes. Strieber describes his feelings:

> That voice had been so final, so absolutely authoritative, and so implacable. Suddenly I realized what was happening: That was a gigantic unknown object up there, and my son must be in it. I had interrupted the visitors in the middle of one of their abductions.[22]

There was nothing Strieber could do about it. He returned forlornly to the cabin, feeling "furious and totally impotent." Trudging obediently upstairs, he immediately fell asleep on his bed. The next morning Strieber was awakened by the sound of his son bounding cheerfully up the stairs to their room as if nothing unusual had happened during the night.

Except for one thing. As Strieber recounts it, his son "seemed filled with a new light of the mind." Indeed, the youngster began spouting Eastern-mystical rhetoric, making statements such as "Reality is God's dream" and "The unconscious is like the universe beyond the quasars."[23]

Strieber realized that his young son could not have come up with such ideas on his own, and was profoundly moved, probably because these statements express the same pantheistic philosophy that emerges on the pages of his books. The idea that his son was abducted and indoctrinated by aliens seems in retrospect to have caused little consternation, perhaps because Strieber persists in believing in the goodness and wisdom of the alien abductors, though it flies in the face of his bizarre, terrifying experiences.

Incredibly, Strieber remains a true believer in his aliens even after encounters like the following, in which he awakened in the night with the realization that, once again, he had been visited by a repulsive creature with arms and legs "like the limbs of a great insect":

> I caught a glimpse of someone crouching just behind my bed-side table. I could see by the huge, dark eyes who it was. I felt an absolutely indescribable sense of menace. It was hell on earth to be there, and yet I couldn't move, couldn't cry out, couldn't get away. I lay as still as death, suffering inner agonies. Whatever was there seemed so monstrously ugly, so filthy, and dark and sinister. Of course they were demons. They had to be.[24]

Can anyone read such descriptions and honestly contend that whatever was lurking beside Whitley Strieber's bed that night was *good?* Yet, as incomprehensible as it seems, Strieber continues to maintain that these monstrous entities are benevolent.

How can this be? My guess is that Strieber, along with the vast majority of UFO researchers, simply has no other option but to trust in the ultimate goodness of the aliens. The alternative—to admit the possibility that they are evil—would be to confess the unthinkable: that the biblical worldview about supernatural reality is true.

Conclusion

Blind dogmatism cannot overpower truth. There is little evidence, as we have seen, to support the idea that UFOs originate from distant planets. In fact, there is every reason to believe they are non-physical entities that inhabit another dimension parallel to our own. Furthermore, they give every indication of being hostile toward the human race. And their connection with occultism is unmistakable.

In short, they are what the Bible calls the "rulers," the "authorities" and "the spiritual forces of evil in the heavenly realms."

Examples from previous chapters indicate that entities thought to be angels can also fit into this nefarious category. Whether false angel or UFO alien, the goal is the same: the transformation of consciousness. Men and women are being deceived into accepting a non-Christian worldview. And for what purpose? The way is being prepared for the ultimate appearance of the Antichrist.

Let us now examine exactly *how* these aliens are able to deceive their helpless victims into accepting their twisted perversion of spiritual truth.

6

Analysis of a Phenomenon

S
o far we have seen that, with regard to UFOs and their accompanying aliens, the smoking gun leads directly to demonic activity. Let us now assemble some observations to help us understand the phenomenon.

First, not all that glitters in the night sky is from another dimension. UFO researchers believe that only a small percentage of sightings of unusual objects can be considered possible UFOs. The J. Allen Hynek Center for UFO Studies has investigated more than one hundred thousand sightings from around the world. Only about five percent cannot be explained as either natural phenomena or man-made objects. Similarly, the Mutual UFO Network (MUFON) estimates that less than ten percent of all sightings are legitimate UFOs.

This does not mean that upwards of ten percent of all sightings are actual aliens or spaceships. The term *UFO* simply means "unidentified flying object." Many of these UFOs can be either natural phenomena or manmade objects that for one reason or another have not yet been identified.

When all is said and done, however, there remains a residual of occurrences—numbering in the many thousands—that defy rational explanation. But when dealing with UFO phenomena, even the meaning of the term *rational* comes into question. Reading the accounts of Whitley Strieber and others, one has the sense of wandering through a subjective maze of the author's disconnected thought processes. Did the events described *really* happen? Strieber, in the midst of telling his bizarre story, admits to having fabricated elaborate incidents in the past. So why should we believe him now?[1]

To complicate matters, Jacques Vallee rails against "true believer" investigators willing to consider only the evidence that supports their own biased ideas:

> It is at this point that the very people who could help us in our investigation, namely the UFO researchers themselves, become caught up in their own need to believe in the most bizarre theories, for which not a shred of real proof exists.[2]

This is the main reason, according to Vallee, that legitimate researchers have largely deserted the field: They have become disenchanted with the absence of level-headed thinking and rigorous scientific analysis.

The Hidden Agenda

The more you read the UFO abduction literature, the more it appears to represent a religious search for the meaning of human existence. Whitley Strieber turns to Eastern mysticism to explain his experience, while Raymond Fowler and Budd Hopkins cling to the genetic manipulation theory, by which the origin of man is explained by alien intervention.

Even ostensibly objective researchers like historian Dr. David M. Jacobs of Temple University, Pulitzer Prize-winning psychiatrist John E. Mack of Harvard Medical School and psychologist Dr. Edith Fiore have their own not-so-hidden agendas. Each in turn refuses to admit anything inherently evil about the phenomenon. Jacobs has embraced the fantastic genetic alteration idea whereby aliens are here to collect human sperm and eggs in order to create and incubate hybrid alien-human fetuses. Mack looks to mystical philosophy to elucidate the hybrid theory. Fiore encourages her readers to use occult means such as a pendulum to "discover your own close encounter."[3]

Oddly, despite differences in their theories, no fundamental disagreement exists. Each of the three researchers considers all life (whether human or alien) to have developed through natural processes; and, more importantly, believes in a universe without God as understood in the Judeo-Christian sense of the word. In fact, each writer's position is compatible with the occult-mystical worldview as expressed in Hinduism, Buddhism and other Eastern religions, known in philosophical terms as pantheism or monism.

So we might ask: If many UFO investigators are actually promoting their own views of ultimate reality, and casting suspicion, for that reason, on the objectivity of their research, should the whole lot be dismissed as mere occult-mystical propaganda?

Not quite. Even someone as jaded and disenchanted about the state of UFO research as Jacques Vallee is forced to conclude that there is *something* behind all the hype:

> In my opinion the evidence is very strong that a genuine UFO phenomenon exists, but serious, dedicated, and aggressive

research is required to peel away this first layer and to find
the real facts.[4]

Entrapped by Dark Angels

A verse in 2 Timothy, which has generally been interpreted symbolically, may speak of a reality that until
recent times would have been too incredible to fathom:

> ... They will come to their senses and escape from the trap
> of the devil, who has taken them captive to do his will.
>
> 2 Timothy 2:26

We have already seen that UFO and alien phenomena
have close links to the occult and what the Bible calls "the
dominion of darkness," inhabited by evil spirits and
demons. Far from being the mischievous elves of medieval
folklore, these evil beings possess an ancient intelligence
and cunning far eclipsing that of mortal man. In addition,
the New Testament warns that these evil forces and their
minions can perform supernatural wonders that would
"deceive even the elect—if that were possible" (Matthew
24:24). Furthermore, we see in the book of Revelation
that the supreme leader of the evil forces known as the
devil will one day bring a great deception on mankind
(Revelation 19:20; 20:10).

The evidence suggests, as we assemble the pieces of the
puzzle so far, that incredibly intelligent and hostile entities from a parallel dimension are perpetrating on the
human race a deception of cosmic proportions. One
aspect of that demonic deception involves otherworldly
encounters with aliens.

The description in 2 Timothy of those being taken captive by malevolent spiritual forces is an uncannily accurate description of what actually transpires during a typical abduction sequence. Psychiatrist John Mack, in his

study of close encounters entitled *Abduction: Human Encounters with Aliens,* describes how individuals find themselves unable to resist the will of the aliens. It is as if they have been paralyzed by invisible chains while they are being captured:

> Abductees may still be able to move their heads, and usually they can see what is going on, although frequently they will close their eyes so they can deny or avoid experiencing the reality of what is occurring. The terror associated with this helplessness blends with the frightening nature of the whole strange experience.[5]

But how exactly does it work? Let's look at some of the possible mechanics involved in taking abductees captive.

Inside or Outside the Mind?

One puzzling question is whether the deception functions on an *external* or *internal* level. Are evil spirits able to manufacture actual physical objects that can be seen in the sky and into which people are abducted? Or, conversely, do demonic forces project images into the mind that lead people to *believe* they are experiencing these things?

A definitive answer to this question is impossible, simply because the very entities we would need to query are uncooperative and by their very nature inveterate liars. It is fruitless and even dangerous to think otherwise (a trap that some have unfortunately fallen into). Nevertheless, from what evidence is available to us, it seems that spirits from the demonic world are able to effect a mixture of both external and internal realities.

With regard to external manifestations, such effects to occultists are not only possible but familiar. Photographs of "ghosts" and materialized objects have long been the subjects of curiosity and study. One little-known phenomenon is the temporary formation of objects out of a mysterious substance called ectoplasm, which some occultists claim to have produced during séances:

> [Ectoplasm is] a subtle living matter present in the physical body primarily invisible but capable of assuming vaporous liquid or solid states and properties. . . . [It] is the substance out of which materialized forms are built by the spirit operators. . . . Ectoplasm has been photographed on many occasions and appears opaque white by infra-red flashlight which is the usual method employed.[6]

This psychic substance is allegedly drawn out of a medium's body while he or she is under trance and formed by the evil spirits into objects that are clearly visible. Ectoplasm is temporary in nature and, according to reports, dissolves of its own accord. If the medium is disturbed and the ectoplasm is suddenly withdrawn back into the body, it can cause serious physical damage.

Whether or not ectoplasm actually exists is an open question. The Bible indicates, however, that evil spirits indeed have the power to form objects. When Aaron threw his staff down in front of Pharaoh, for example, the Egyptian occultists were able to duplicate the miracle:

> Pharaoh then summoned wise men and sorcerers, and the Egyptian magicians also did the same things by their secret arts: Each one threw down his staff and it became a snake. But Aaron's staff swallowed up their staffs.
>
> Exodus 7:11–12

The Egyptian sorcerers were also able to duplicate the next two miracles performed by Moses and Aaron— changing the Nile water to blood (7:22) and covering the land with frogs (8:7)—although, significantly, they were soon outclassed by the power of the living God working through Moses and Aaron. On other occasions pagan sorcerers were unable to stand up against the true prophet of God. The impotence of the prophets of Baal during the contest with Elijah on Mount Carmel (1 Kings 18:16–40) serves as a prime example.

Still, is it possible that in our day evil spirits are using some diabolical technology similar to that employed by the Egyptian sorcerers? Could that involve using a substance like ectoplasm to "form" UFOs? The point is, demonic spirits have dark powers of which we humans are ignorant, and they are capable somehow of temporarily materializing what are actually only quasi-physical objects. UFO researchers have long suspected that this is the case:

> In 1967 UFO investigator John A. Keel realized that behind the illusory spacecraft there lurked "the real phenomenon," what he termed the "soft objects," i.e., "sightings of transparent or translucent objects seemingly capable of altering their size and shape dramatically." He added that "most of these 'objects' are temporary manipulations of matter and energy."[7]

If UFOs are indeed quasi-physical objects or spiritual manifestations, they are not necessarily subject to the laws of physics. This explains why they have been clocked at speeds several times faster than that of any known jet aircraft while executing maneuvers judged by modern aerodynamics to be virtually impossible.

Also significant is the fact that UFOs seem to operate within a limited time span. The majority of sightings last only a few seconds or, at most, a few minutes, with only the rare exception visible for an hour or longer. If UFOs are indeed temporary spiritual manifestations, we might expect that they could be "constituted" for only limited periods of time.

Why are they temporary? Perhaps this is part of the divinely ordained limits placed on demonic activity. After all, if such phenomena were allowed to operate without restraint, imagine the unlimited terror that evil spirits would be able to inflict on mankind! One day, according to the book of Revelation, this is exactly what will happen. Later we will see how UFO phenomena might be one aspect of that demonic terror.

As to why some UFOs are manifested longer than others, it might have something to do with who sees them. There is evidence in the 1947 Mount Rainier incident of a conscious interaction between UFOs and their observers. UFO researcher Paul Devereux, in investigating a related phenomenon known as earthlights, discovered indications of this:

> There are indications that the type of unusual energy forming earthlight events may be sensitive to consciousness; that the interaction between witness and light might be truly two-way. Dr. Harley D. Rutledge, investigating lights in a mountainous area of southern Missouri in the late 1970's, notes that there were cases in which lights "may have reacted" to the thoughts or subtle actions of team members, including himself.[8]

A mysterious phenomenon during World War II caused considerable anxiety among both Allied and Axis intelligence. Fighter pilots on both sides reported seeing strange light forms maneuvering near their aircraft. These early UFOs were dubbed "foo fighters" by pilots and were feared to be some unknown technical marvel possessed by the other side. Devereux notes that Allied crew members who experienced foo fighters "sometimes complained that the lights seemed to respond to their thoughts."[9] This might help explain why some people seem to attract UFOs.

One of the early and most colorful abductees was George Adamski, who claimed to have ventured with his alien friends to most of the planets of our solar system. UFO researcher Dennis Stacy notes:

> In August 1947, on a single night, Adamski watched star-struck as a stream of saucers—a total of 184 by his count—streaked overhead. Not surprisingly, since he was seemingly acting like a lodestone for such things, Adamski began trying to photograph the objects.[10]

As we have seen, however, attempts to photograph UFOs rarely succeed. Despite years of extraordinary claims about his contacts with aliens, Adamski never produced any evidence that would pass rigorous examination. Likewise, numerous attempts by abductees notwithstanding, there exists not a single report of an object successfully removed from inside a UFO attesting to its actual material nature.[11]

Indications that UFOs react to their observers and the lack of tangible evidence suggest that the experience might actually originate from forces operating *within* the human brain. Could it be a case of mind over matter?

Demonic Virtual Reality

We now turn to the question of whether demonic forces can form an artificial reality in the mind.[12] This illusory "virtual reality" would, if possible, deceive the abductee into thinking he or she was actually being transported to an alien spacecraft. According to UFO researcher Jenny Randles, evidence exists suggesting that the abduction experience "is occurring in an altered state of consciousness, and makes one wonder if, in a situation where a witness is supposedly abducted from his car (e.g., police officer Alan Godfrey), they ever *really* get out of the vehicle at all."[13]

Such a capacity for artificial reality, which we experience to varying degrees when we dream, seems to exist naturally in our brains. Many people can recall dreams so lifelike and vivid that, in the midst of the dream itself, they wondered whether they were actually asleep. Is it possible that demonic entities, possessing vastly superior intelligence in combination with paranormal abilities, are able to manipulate this natural capacity and mimic reality within the human brain?

Significantly, the majority of close encounters with UFOs occur at night when the abductee is either asleep or functioning at a lower level of alertness. Whitley Strieber laments the fact that the aliens "have continued to come to me only late at night or in the predawn hours," the effect of which is "to deliver us into their hands in a completely helpless state."[14]

It is possible that some abduction experiences, particularly when the subject is awakened from sleep or experiences an OBE, may actually be the equivalent of a vivid dream or vision. These virtual reality experiences could be engineered and magnified by demonic forces inside the abductee's brain, involving the manipulation of each of the five senses in such a way as to convince the abductee that he or she is being transported physically to another location.

Abductees usually insist that their experiences really happened. But their written transcripts and written accounts of abductions often seem disjointed and have an air of unreality. A scene is described—for example, the interior of a UFO craft—with only a few isolated and confusing details, far less than would be recalled during a similar incident during waking hours commanding the same degree of interest. In the dream state our minds tend to have a narrow range of focus, so that on waking we remember certain details without the breadth of awareness we possess while awake.

Also, in abduction sequences the focus typically changes quickly and involves shifts of time and space that would be impossible in three-dimensional reality. One outlandish scene is followed by another, as the subject is led through a dreamlike, ethereal netherworld. As David Jacobs writes:

> From the first few seconds of an abduction, nothing is within the realm of normal human experience. It is an instant descent into the fantastic and bizarre. Technology and biotechnology that seem like magic are immediately apparent. Once the event begins, humans are powerless to stop it.[15]

Still, the abduction experience cannot be reduced to merely a demonically engineered virtual reality. The memories of even the most harrowing of dreams slowly but surely fade away, and later recollections usually lack the element of profound, immediate terror. The fright of abduction experiences, by contrast, often remains with the abductee for years afterwards, and if recalled through hypnotic regression becomes once again vivid and terrifying. In this sense, abduction experiences more closely resemble horrific human experiences like assault or rape than dreaming.

Factors like the unexplained appearance of physical injuries and scars on the bodies of abductees also suggest that something real occurred. And sightings of UFOs by multiple observers indicate that, at least in such cases, the phenomenon does not originate solely in one person's mind.

Thus, it is reasonable to conclude that UFO sightings and abductions may be quasi-real experiences engineered by demonic forces by means of metaphysical abilities about which we simply have no knowledge. They are profoundly deceptive experiences that likely involve both manipulation of external reality and the subject's internal perceptions of reality. However we explain it, the abduction experience is in a very real sense the terrifying sense of being taken captive by hostile entities.

Secret Longings

Now we come to the most ominous aspect of the explosion of UFO sightings and abduction cases that began in the late 1940s and continues unabated to the present day: its connection with future events predicted by biblical prophecy. There is a sinister reason why growing numbers of individuals are being "taken captive" by demonic forces.

Sifting through the numerous published accounts of abductions at the hands of alien creatures, it is hard not to be startled by the abductee's reaction. Rather than being revulsed by their abductors, or in addition to revulsion, all too often they express positive emotions—even feelings of love toward the aliens.

After all Whitley Strieber suffered at the hands of the aliens—suffering he describes in the most horrific of terms—he repeatedly confesses his strong attraction to them:

> They were so terrible, so ugly, so fierce, and I was so small and helpless. I could smell that odor of theirs like a greasy smoke hanging in my nostrils. Again, though, I felt love. Despite all the ugliness and the terrible things that had been done, I found myself longing for them, missing them! How was this possible?[16]

Indeed, how *is* it possible for abductees to have a reaction that flies in the face of the reality of their experience? John Mack offers a bizarre explanation: It is part of the necessary "bonding process" taking place between humans and aliens:

> The connection that human beings experience through looking into the eyes of the aliens seems to be a central feature of the acknowledgment of the existence of the beings and the establishment of the bond itself. Abductees have repeatedly described to me a loving, totally engulfing feeling they experience when they look into these huge, black, all-knowing eyes.[17]

We should pause here to note that, with regard to abduction research, the adage *Consider the source* is vitally important. It is fair to point out, while not questioning anyone's professional credentials, that researchers in this field (virtually to a man) reject belief in Satan and demonic forces. Thus, though it is impossible to completely suppress the negative evidence about the aliens, they employ a herculean effort to "put a human face" on what are obviously abhorrent entities.

In any case, while the aliens are clearly not the benevolent, all-wise creatures they are presented as, they do hold a certain macabre attraction for many abductees. The reason lies in the occult-mystical worldview that (as we have seen) is connected with UFO abduction phenomena.

Ultimate reality, according to this fundamentally anti-Christian worldview, lies not in the personal, triune God presented in the Bible. Rather, the universe itself is divine, a manifestation of what is loosely termed *God*. According to the occult-mystical worldview, however, God is a wholly impersonal force that might be likened to the understanding by modern physics of energy.

Emotive concepts such as love are routinely—and arbitrarily—injected into the cold, impersonal universe of Eastern mysticism in order to soften the devastating implications for the meaning of life. There is, in truth, no meaning—only the loss of human personality and inevitable "reabsorption into the void." Thus, we have John Mack's use of meaningful terminology to make a purposeless worldview more palatable:

> The connecting principle, the force that expands our consciousness beyond ourselves, appears to be love. In the discovery of a fundamental, loving interconnectedness, we might overcome the sense of fragmentation and evolve towards wholeness. . . . The earth would become the jewel in the crown of our being, the place where we experience once again our connection with a cosmic Source from which we have become too separate.[18]

Mack, et al., notwithstanding, the pretension that the aliens have anything to do with genuine love is illusory; such entities are incapable of virtue. The real hook that draws their victims is the age-old promise of immortality, as in Robert Fowler's alien who pointed to the starry sky and promised, "You yourself will see the universe as I have seen it."[19]

We need only turn to the Bible to discover the source of such spurious promises. The initial deception faced by humankind was that of the serpent's offer of divinity: "You will be like God, knowing good and evil" (Genesis 3:5). This false, unattainable temptation has remained the primary goal of the non-theistic religions of the world. And now, at the end of the twentieth century, we are seeing the very deception coming to us in a fantastically advanced configuration. Jacques Vallee speaks of the potential for delusion:

More importantly, the UFO mystery holds a mirror to our own fantasies, it expresses our secret longings for a wisdom that might come down from the stars in new, improved, easy-to-use packaging, to reveal the secrets of life and tell us, at long last, who we are.[20]

This, I believe, is precisely why the public, while remaining "officially" skeptical, is entranced by the possibilities offered by UFO phenomena. It may also explain why abductees suffer gladly all too often the cruel bonds of captivity by evil beings.

Something in the Air

The stage is being set for a confrontation of cosmic proportions between radically opposed forces. On the one side is the witness of the Christian Church to the one true God and to the truths of Scripture ably summarized by the Apostles' Creed:

I believe in God the Father Almighty, maker of heaven and earth; and in Jesus Christ his only Son our Lord: who was conceived by the Holy Spirit, born of the Virgin Mary, suffered under Pontius Pilate, was crucified, dead, and buried; he descended into hell; the third day he rose from the dead; he ascended into heaven, and sitteth at the right hand of God the Father Almighty; from thence he shall come to judge the quick and the dead. I believe in the Holy Spirit, the holy catholic Church, the communion of saints, the forgiveness of sins, the resurrection of the body, and the life everlasting. Amen.

This early creed is a brilliant summary of the central beliefs of Christendom, which are profoundly anathema to the enemy, who will stop at nothing to hinder, distort and destroy the truth. So we find that the rhetoric of erudite spokesmen welcoming the alien presence is but a thin veneer masking contempt for Christianity.

It is not surprising that John Mack should comment that the UFO phenomenon "presents a particular problem for some organized religions." Mack goes on to lament the fact that certain "groups of human beings" throughout history, "recognizing the power and potential peril of spirit forces 'out there,' have taken upon themselves the task of guiding us." He decries in particular the "zeal" of the Church during the Middle Ages that, while seeking to "impose a particular sort of monotheism based on the Trinity, quite ruthlessly suppressed the nature-worshiping polytheism of much of Europe." This to Mack was a tragic development, in that expressions of paganism and Eastern religions are more accepting of UFO aliens and their message for mankind. But in admitting this he makes a fascinating observation:

> Eastern religious traditions, such as Tibetan Buddhism, which have always recognized a vast range of spirit entities in the cosmos, seem to have less difficulty accepting the actuality of UFO abduction phenomena than do the more dualistic monotheisms, *which offer powerful resistance to acceptance.*[21]

I hope the Church is prepared to offer vigorous opposition to the coming powerful deception by alien UFO "spiritual forces of evil in the heavenly realms" (Ephesians 6:12). There does appear to be something in the air. Statistics about numbers of UFO sightings and alien abductions worldwide give every indication that the forces of darkness are gradually *increasing* their overt contact with humankind. Is the stage even now being prepared for the end-time deception?

The Alien-Controlled Fifth Column

An ominous specter looms on the horizon: that of growing numbers of individuals programmed, either con-
sciously or subconsciously, to accept a future alien UFO
manifestation in the world. Speculates Raymond Fowler
not altogether unapprovingly, "How many thousands (perhaps hundreds of thousands) of people walking the streets
are being monitored, controlled, and preconditioned to
accept (even *welcome*) large-scale overt contact?"[22]

Up until now the UFO and abduction phenomena take
place largely at night and are unable to manifest themselves openly for extended periods. But what if that were
to change? Imagine the pandemonium that would break
out if the world were to see astonishing televised images
of UFOs disgorging aliens with their "message" for
mankind!

It is difficult, admittedly, to envision large segments of
the population accepting and welcoming aliens. But consider an incident that occurred on a Los Angeles television show in 1982. A UFO investigator of dubious credentials quoted from an alleged interplanetary message
for mankind. The alien statement was remarkable only
for its banality, merely repeating the kind of ecological
warning that respected scientists have been voicing for
decades. Nevertheless, as Vallee notes, the show brought
a tidal wave of response from viewers:

> The reaction to the broadcast was immediate. The station
> was flooded with calls. Hundreds of people requested copies
> of the message, all over southern California. The station had
> to read it on the air again for two weeks to allow people to
> record it. Some of the callers were crying.[23]

While stopping short of endorsing the view that UFOs
and aliens are inherently evil, Vallee is one researcher who

has dared to broach the possibility. He makes a profound suggestion—that the UFO phenomenon might well consist of "actual beings" who are "staging simulated operations, very much in the manner of a theatrical play or movie, in order to release into our culture certain images that will influence us toward a goal we are incapable of perceiving" (pp. 176–177).

Vallee warns that the more we pursue abduction research, naively accepting certain assumptions about the aliens' intentions, the more we "play *their* game and reinforce the artificially projected imagery." That false imagery includes dogmatic beliefs regarding both the physical appearance and purposes of the aliens:

> The American public is being taught to expect an imminent landing by extraterrestrials and to recognize them as short, gray aliens with big dark eyes. . . . The fact that real UFO witnesses actually describe a wide variety of other shapes has been censored, to such an extent that some research groups do not even accept these other shapes into their database.
>
> pages 177, 288

One day the world at large may indeed witness a mind-boggling public manifestation of UFOs and their alien occupants. If and when such an event occurs, there will be little doubt as to the message they will bring. Undoubtedly many nominal Christians will attempt to view such an unsettling event in religious terms. Not a few will follow abductee Betty Andreasson in believing that this is what is meant by the Second Coming of Christ.[24]

Which raises a provocative question: Will such religiously oriented individuals be assisted in their deception by "angelic" beings?

Angelic Aliens

In earlier chapters we examined various kinds of spiritual phenomena that have excited considerable popular interest. We have seen the fine line distinguishing possibly genuine angelic visitations from their clever, manipulative counterfeits. Betty Eadie's experience, for example, included the well-known "tunnel of light" through which she supposedly traveled before being met by a glorious spirit creature she calls "Jesus."

The differences between Eadie's experience and alien abductions seem at first glance to be profound. After all, Eadie reports an overwhelmingly positive experience in a heavenly region of light and happiness; whereas abductees typically recall terror in loathsome settings at the hands of frightening beings. But let's recall the biblical warning that evil forces can present themselves "as angels of light." Can there be subtle similarities between the angelic and the alien experience?

Surprisingly, they agree in significant aspects. Psychiatrist John Mack describes what often occurs during the abduction sequence. Of particular interest is the fact that "spirit beings" are present and thought to mediate between the individual and "God":

> The aliens are recognized as intermediaries or intermediate beings between . . . human beings and the primal source of creation or God (in the sense of a cosmic consciousness, rather than a personified being). In this regard abductees sometimes liken the alien beings to angels. . . ."[25]

Betty Eadie's account also involves spirit beings that guide her during her time in the spirit world. While she speaks of God, she provides no clear definition of what she means, nor does she claim to have seen God at any time during her heavenly visit.

Curiously, while the majority of abductees have highly unpleasant, even terrifying experiences, this is not always the case. Some abductees recall being transported to a place that elicits positive emotions:

> The abductees may actually experience themselves as returning to their cosmic source or "Home," an inexpressibly beautiful realm beyond, or not in, space/time as we know it. . . . Conversely, abductees may weep with sadness [at] having to leave their cosmic home, return to Earth and become embodied once again.[26]

Similarly, Betty Eadie speaks of crying and begging not to be sent back when told she must return: "Without hesitation, I said, 'No, no. I can't go back. I belong here. This is my home.'" Upon returning to the hospital, still in spirit form, she gazes down with revulsion at her earthly body: "I felt like I had just taken a long, soothing shower, and now I had to put that heavy, cold, muddy garment on."[27]

The obvious differences between the experiences of Betty Eadie and Whitley Strieber make any comparison seem contrived. But we must return to the scriptural warning about demonic forces appearing as angels of light. As improbable as it seems, even those who claim to have had favorable experiences may have been taken captive and deceived by evil powers. In the case of Betty Eadie, the decisive factor is that the teachings of her spirit guides are in clear opposition to the Bible.

Conclusion

Professor David Jacobs mentions the wide variety of forms that the abduction experience may take:

> Many other abductions have been couched in personal and cultural terms—visits from deceased relatives, encounters

with angels, devils, and other religious figures, mystical meetings with animals, out-of-body experiences, and so on.[28]

I have already suggested that deceptive angelic encounters, as well as alien abductions, are actually a process whereby the individual is taken captive by demonic forces. As we evaluate seemingly positive experiences, we must examine how the individual is affected spiritually. It is evident that both ecstatic and horrific abductions are used by evil powers to accomplish the same purpose: spiritual transformation leading to the rejection of the true God.

Growing evidence indicates that both angelic and alien abductions are being used with great effect presently to lure multitudes of converts to a counterfeit worldview that promises immortality and divinity to men and women. This seductive deception is rapidly gaining the ascendancy in Western society, as it has long predominated in the East. Is it even possible for the human race to resist the angelic and alien subterfuge? Some will doubtless agree with Vallee's pessimistic assessment: "Perhaps we have no choice."[29]

But there is more to the story: The Bible states there will be many who will overcome Satan "by the blood of the Lamb and by the word of their testimony" (Revelation 12:11). These overcomers will recognize false angels and aliens as emissaries of that mysterious figure of human history—the leader of the final revolt against God known as the Antichrist.

It is to this enigmatic personage that we now turn.

Part 2

Antichrist Past and Present

7

The Mysterious "Organization X"

Is the diabolical personage known as the Antichrist in our very midst today, lurking somewhere behind the scenes waiting to be revealed? This was one of the burning questions for which I hoped to find answers as I entered the church auditorium in eager anticipation of the prophetic Bible conference taught by a nationally known prophecy teacher.

The session that evening was billed "Mr. 666—Antichrist—Who? When?" It was the stuff of cloak and dagger, and I found myself captivated by the fascinating tidbits revealed during the message about the coming Man of Sin. Later, during a private conversation in which I felt honored to be taken into the itinerant preacher's confidence, more details emerged. Specifically I was informed about a sinister, arcane conspiracy headed by an elusive figure referred to only as "Mr. X."

The teacher opened bulging files stuffed with clippings, articles and other evidence to support his contention of a sinister plot to bring the world under satanic domination. I was impressed and sensed I was being initiated into the deeper mysteries behind world history. Books were recommended, names were dropped, and before we parted a reprint of an article entitled simply (and ominously) "Organization X" was thrust into my hands.

On returning home I devoured the article. It spoke of a clandestine satanic organization possessing immense power and resources, operating with impunity to influence the course of world affairs. Few people, it contended, including Christians, were aware of it. My mind reeled. It was as though my eyes had been opened to Machiavellian forces next to which the intrigues of the CIA or KGB paled in comparison. They were child's play; this worldwide diabolic conspiracy eclipsed them all.

It is impossible to describe the transformation that I underwent beginning that evening. It led to a personal investigation lasting many years as I explored a previously unknown dark, hidden side of world events—a history parallel to that found in history books, one that claimed to offer the interpretive key to the enigmas of international politics.

The source of the article given to me was an obscure publication out of England called *The Intelligence Digest* that specialized in tracking the movements of the alleged worldwide plot. The prophecy teacher cautioned me that the editor awarded subscriptions capriciously; and indeed, while I managed to ascertain that such a publication existed, I never managed to get on the mailing list. Apparently I was not judged worthy to be granted access to the privileged information revealed on the pages of *The Intelligence Digest*. This only confirmed my newfound belief that an impenetrable worldwide conspiracy, and now a counter-conspiracy, actually existed.

But back to the story of the enigmatic Mr. X, a man presented as very likely none other than the yet-to-be-revealed Antichrist. The article, written in the terse style of an intelligence report, describes this individual matter-of-factly:

> It would be unwise to say too much about this at present. However, some details can be given. The head of this organization looks about 40. In all probability he is very much older. He speaks a large number of languages, is very musical, and extremely handsome. His intellectual attainments are of the highest order. He had [sic] no known father or mother. He is not married and has no children. His charm is very great. He changes his name and appearance frequently. He has recently been in Moscow and Peking. His visits to Rome are very frequent. . . . He has a peculiar liking for corpses. . . . Oddly enough, though driven by ambition and often very successful, he is of a deeply pessimistic nature and said to be convinced of his ultimate failure. His wealth is immense. In the arts he favors the grotesque. He is afraid of certain things, although otherwise intrepid.[1]

This personage is referred to in the article as the head of a covert organization called "Force X":

> The numerical size of his organization is not known. But it is very large and, on the whole, all those employed make a great deal of money, but do not end up in such comfortable circumstances as they enjoy during their heyday. Disillusion seems to dog the steps of his agents after awhile.

The agents of Force X are said to be spread like an invisible dragnet around the globe:

> Our investigations disclose a diversified group which has worldwide links. This group seems to believe that it is so

strong that it can afford to use Communism without danger that the Communists will, in consequence, eliminate it; and that it can afford to use the homosexual movement (which is very powerful) without rotting civilization. . . .

Over the years this group has enlisted disgruntled intellectuals, those with a grudge against the old order of society, those in financial need, and those with vices. It has bought up large interests in publishing concerns, in the film industry, in financial houses, and in other institutions. It has devoted immense attention to detail, so that it now controls vital things in every sphere.

The article paints a picture of an organization wielding almost unbelievable power:

This force, which we can call "X," is closely-coordinated. It is of one mind; it is in control of immense resources; it is convinced, passionate, efficient, and deadly. It fears only one thing—public opinion. It tries to control this and to stop anyone from arousing it. The leaders of this force occupy positions of the highest respectability. . . .

As described, this Force X has a seamy underside, with its well-placed agents around the world involved in illegal ventures:

This person is a great expert on Africa and an orientalist in the bargain. His agents have made huge sums from the drug trade, which he encourages. He has many Jewish agents, but detests Israel. His contacts in Latin America are extensive. In western Europe, he reckons Germany to be his best field.

Intriguing details about the attitude of X toward leading figures in evangelical Christianity are also revealed:

His personal hatreds are intense and he seems to pick on certain people in particular. For example, he loathes Dr. Billy

Graham with an intensity extraordinary to watch. He has been present at some of Dr. Graham's meetings and has tried to infiltrate the Graham organization—not very successfully.

An odd disclosure! It reminded me of the Bible's portrayal of the Antichrist as the mortal enemy of Christians. As for the motivation behind this elusive individual:

This is the most difficult question to answer. Indeed, we doubt if he could himself fully supply the answer. It would not be difficult to think that in the last analysis this person is mad; but, if so, dangerously so. Although much that he is doing involves risk of war, it is known that he greatly fears this. He does not want war, but power without taking the risk.

Anticipating the obvious question as to why no government has taken action against this subversive organization, the article provides an alarming answer:

This group is not recognized by authority because authority is afraid to investigate too closely. The rot has gone too deep; too many are involved. No government will ever investigate.

There you have it. It sounded almost too alarming to be true yet gave every indication of being a deadly serious report about Force X and its mysterious leader. And did it not echo what the Bible teaches about a supremely powerful and demonically inspired individual suddenly bursting on the world scene at the end of time?

My Own Journey

Thus was I compelled to begin my prolonged study of the subject. It led me first (at the prophecy teacher's recommendation) to the reading of classic treatments such as Gary Allen's *None Dare Call It Conspiracy* and Nesta

Webster's *World Conspiracy*, in which I found the general outlines of world conspiracy theory. Through Professor James Robison's eighteenth-century treatise on the Illuminati, I learned that the roots went far deeper, originating in Bavaria on the European continent.

A wealth of conspiracy literature was opened up to me, including monthly publications such as *American Opinion* and *The American Mercury*. I learned about powerful, secretive organizations like the Council on Foreign Relations, the Trilateral Commission and the Bilderburger Society. These were said to be linked for the purpose of bringing about a "New World Order"—the notorious buzzword that has become so familiar to American evangelicals. Books popular in Christian circles like the now-discredited *Satan Seller* by Mike Warnke purported to relate the devilish aspects of the alleged conspiracy.

There was no end to the ever-deepening layers of intrigue, suspicion cast upon organizations, well-known political and religious figures, powerful banks and international corporations—until at long last I sensed the whole incredible edifice tottering from its own weight.

It is beyond the scope of this book to present a detailed critique of various conspiracy theories and their influence on current Bible prophecy teachings. (For those interested, my evaluation of a recent popular book, *Dark Majesty* by Texe Marrs, appears in the appendix.) What I *can* share with the reader is my personal evaluation based on many years of fascination with the subject. I embarked on my study not skeptical but eager to discover any correlation between the often inexplicable events of our world with biblical prophecy.

It was not difficult for me to become a true believer in conspiracy theories. After all, doesn't the Bible teach that the Antichrist will come, and isn't it at least possible that we are living in the last days? If so, then the Antichrist is surely alive somewhere in the world today. And since his identity is not yet revealed, isn't it logical to assume that he is already operating behind the scenes, influencing world events in preparation for the day of his unveiling?

So *voilà*, there you have it—a perfectly rational basis for believing that the world is in the grip of an unimaginably powerful yet unseen satanic conspiracy.

What, then, turned sour? In my case, after extensive reading over a period of time, I gradually saw the inner contradictions of the conspiracy theories. Let me offer an example going back to the 1970s.

At that time it was claimed, repeatedly and assuredly, that the presidency of Jimmy Carter had been engineered by the "internationalists"—a code word for the unseen network of bankers and industrialists bent on world domination. Much was made of Carter's meteoric rise from peanut farming in Georgia to the most powerful political office on earth. How could this have happened had he not been propelled to such heights by powerful individuals pulling the strings behind the scenes? His administration was seen by the conspiracy theorists as a triumph of the Trilateral Commission and the Council on Foreign Relations. Now it was feared that they would have free rein to implement their designs for a one-world, anti-Christian political system.

Particular attention was directed toward President Carter's flamboyant and uncannily successful Secretary of State, Henry Kissinger. To add fuel to the fire, Kissinger's name was induced by prophecy teachers to yield the magical numerical value of 666.

The turn of events, however, did not support the grandiose claims of the conspiracy writers. Four years later Jimmy Carter lost his bid for reelection. Kissinger's political career also sputtered to a halt.

Observing the trouncing of the Carter administration at the polls, I remember wondering what happened to the so-called invincible powers backing them. They did not turn out to be so omnipotent after all.

Not to worry. The conspiracists were ready with the next scenario. No sooner had Jimmy Carter returned home to Plains, Georgia, when the focus of the attack was shifted to the new president, Ronald Reagan. Now it was the ex-governor of California who was actually the stooge of the one-worlders and who would bring about their nefarious program. After all, weren't virtually all of the members of his Cabinet also members of the Council on Foreign Relations?

And so it went. After Reagan it was George Bush who, with his Ivy League background and connections with Big Oil, would lead America down the path to godless, anti-Christian ruin. Bush's membership in an obscure club called Skull and Bones while an undergraduate at Yale University decades earlier was cited as evidence of his true pagan self. But somehow George Bush's promotion of a New World Order could not prevent his defeat at the polls at the end of his first term.

Bush's successor, former Arkansas governor Bill Clinton, then became the target of the same conspiracy theorists. His success in promoting both NAFTA (the North American Free Trade Agreement) and GATT (the worldwide General Agreement on Tariffs and Trade) led to grave suspicion that he was secretly bringing about the one-world economic system controlled by the Antichrist.

I began to notice a recurring pattern in which the same shadowy conspiracy is ascribed to the current political leader, who is described in terms suggestive of the Antichrist. When the dire predictions fail to materialize, attention is deftly switched to the next person in power. This is because by its very nature the "conspiracy" remains behind the scenes and thus immune from scrutiny.

Remarkable claims can be made that are by definition impossible to verify—or disprove.

Mr. X—The End of the Story

Let's return to our account of Force X and its intriguing leader as an example of clandestine plots and Antichrist candidates that fail to pan out. We can conclude with near certainty that the previously described article was bogus—and here's why. As I said earlier, I was given the article while attending a Bible prophecy conference, but for reasons that shall soon become clear I did not say *when* it was.

In fact the year was 1977. Close examination of the article shows it was written more than a decade earlier. Not only are there several references to political figures and events dating from that period, but at one point the article refers to the Kennedy Administration in the present tense. If, as the article states, the Antichrist figure X was at least forty and "in all probability . . . very much older," then by the mid–1990s he would be, at a minimum, *more than seventy years old.*

Few if any portrayals of the Antichrist, however, depict him as a senior citizen. Thus, in this particular case we have the advantage of applying the test of time. Unfortunately several present-day Antichrist candidates proclaimed by prophecy teachers will be inflaming imaginations for some time to come before they are finally (so to speak) laid to rest.

What, then, can we learn from the false promise of Organization X? First let's be clear about one thing: Gullibility and naïveté are not marks of spiritual maturity. We are not to accept every extraordinary claim that we read or hear, but are commanded to exercise our God-given discernment: "Refuse foolish and ignorant speculations, knowing that they produce quarrels" (2 Timothy 2:23, NASB).

As our Organization X story shows, baseless conjecture combined with half-truths can be presented to give a semblance of authenticity. The real mystery, though, is not Force X but why a confessed Christian would write a story about the Antichrist that, at the very least, was not properly corroborated. Whether the author or publisher succumbed to the pressure of holding the interest of the audience by feeding them unproved speculation, or whether they themselves were misled, we may never know.

To Conspire or Not to Conspire?

Does this mean we can all breathe a sigh of relief knowing that there is no Force X conspiracy after all lurking in the shadows? Unfortunately, no. The Scriptures reveal that in the last days of human history the very gates of hell will be opened, unleashing a monstrous evil such as the planet has never known. That evil malignancy, led by the Antichrist, will exercise an unprecedented control over the political, economic and even religious affairs of the world—exactly as the conspiracy theorists claim is happening today.

That having been said, two observations are in order:

1. There is a real danger of escapism. We need to ask ourselves, What is the positive benefit in the ultimately futile effort to uncover and expose such a conspiracy?

Looking back on my own experience, I admit ruefully that my obsession with learning more and more about the alleged diabolical powers only distracted me from more concrete, practical obligations. I found myself engrossed in conspiracy literature that was unrelentingly pessimistic in tone and devoid of edifying value. Spiritually speaking I found the literature to be like empty-calorie sweets that diminished my healthy appetite for the pure Word of God and solid Christian literature. It engendered within me a cynical outlook on life and a suspicious attitude toward others, especially those who did not go along with my conspiracy rhetoric. (That only proved to me that such people were naïve, worldly Christians who would be the first to crumble when the Antichrist was unveiled.) I carried around a subtle chip on my shoulder, thinking I knew the "real" story behind world affairs, when in truth what I had been reading was so confusing and contradictory I scarcely knew which way was up.

2. A wise friend once suggested that, prior to the actual unfolding of the events of Revelation, the worldwide Antichrist conspiracy would be *philosophical-spiritual* rather than *concrete-political*. In other words, we need not postulate the actual existence somewhere in the world of a cadre of shadowy, powerful men headed by the future Antichrist (*à la* the Illuminati) who are manipulating world events behind the scenes. It is not necessary that all occultists, New Age groups and Eastern mystical sects are intertwined organizationally and controlled by the same as-yet-unseen Antichrist and his inner circle.

How then, you might ask, do I explain the fact that these groups seem to espouse the same evil program? The answer is simple: They promote the same New World Order causes because they have a common *belief.* Their unity stems from the fact that their hearts have not been transformed by the Gospel, as Jesus bluntly stated: "You belong to your father, the devil, and you want to carry out your father's desire" (John 8:44).

An illustration from the diversity found among Christians will help explain this. The fact that believers everywhere tend to agree regarding important spiritual issues does not prove that all churches and Christian organizations are directed by some secret inner clique. Christians are united on many basic issues because they have the same Head, the Lord Jesus Christ (Ephesians 1:22–23); the same authority, the Bible (2 Timothy 3:16); and the same teacher, the Holy Spirit, dwelling within them (John 16:13). And it is that same Holy Spirit who gives a marvelous sense of unity that often transcends denominational lines (John 17).

Christians often wonder how the Antichrist will manage to gain such a degree of control over the hearts and minds of unregenerate humankind. The reason is that, having rejected the Gospel of Jesus Christ, they will fall prey instead to the Big Lie:

> The coming of the lawless one will be in accordance with the work of Satan displayed in all kinds of counterfeit miracles, signs and wonders, and in every sort of evil that deceives those who are perishing. They perish because they refused to love the truth and so be saved. For this reason God sends them a powerful delusion so that they will believe the lie.
>
> 2 Thessalonians 2:9–11

Prophecy books and teachings about the identity of the Antichrist, despite having led to much false speculation, continue to offer a certain allure. But are Christians to be unduly preoccupied with such questions in the first place?

In the book of Revelation the apostle John's hand was stayed: "When the seven thunders spoke, I was about to write; but I heard a voice from heaven say, 'Seal up what the seven thunders have said and do not write it down'" (Revelation 10:4). How *fascinating* it would be to know what the seven thunders revealed! But such hidden knowledge has been sealed up. It is not for us to know—and this is surely for our own good. Why should we seek to learn what God has chosen not to reveal to us?

Similarly, the closing verses of the book of Daniel indicate that at least some future prophecies are meant for those living during the time of which they speak: "But you, Daniel, close up and seal the words of the scroll until the time of the end" (Daniel 12:4). In other words, those who are alive when the prophecy comes to pass will be granted supernatural insight into its true interpretation *that we do not currently possess.*

Let there be no doubt about it: There is great value in the careful, informed study of biblical prophecy. The beginning of the Revelation of John promises that "blessed is the one who reads the words of this prophecy, and blessed are those who hear it and take to heart what is written in it, because the time is near" (Revelation 1:3). But hearing God's Word and taking it to heart is a far cry from the supermarket tabloid approach that majors on sensationalism at the expense of mature, balanced contemplation.

It is lamentable that in their sincere desire to see people find salvation in Jesus Christ, certain eager believers advance dubious claims and fabrications that all too often have the long-term effect of discrediting the great truths of biblical prophecy. Ironically, this in itself may prove to be one of the stratagems of the evil one as the time of the end approaches.

Conclusion

Speculation about the identity of the Antichrist and clandestine satanic conspiracies leads to frustration. This is because *by definition* they cannot be revealed, and all efforts to expose them can yield only tantalizing trivia and not solid proof.

The initiate who desires the Gnostic "hidden knowledge" about such things, moreover, must place himself at the mercy of his cryptic sources who alone know the "true" story about what is happening in the world. Chasing after the ever-changing conspiracy theories leads eventually to disillusionment—and a victory for the forces of evil.

In due time the Antichrist and his diabolic program will come; the endless preoccupation with his identity will not alter that one iota. In the meantime Jesus commands us to live in the present, to "seek the Kingdom of God and his righteousness" rather than avoid the present by attempting to escape to the future:

> Therefore do not worry about tomorrow, for tomorrow will worry about itself. Each day has enough trouble of its own.
>
> Matthew 6:34

8

Antichrist in the Bible

Many downright confusing ideas have been propagated concerning the mysterious personage known as the Antichrist. Before we continue negotiating the maze of past and current ideas, let's blow away the chaff and try to determine what the Scripture does and does not say. Surveying the principal passages in the Bible that have to do with the Antichrist will give us a divine perspective by which to evaluate the various candidates who have been suggested throughout history and up to the present time, which we will do in the next three chapters.

Note that as we survey the biblical texts dealing with the coming Antichrist, we will move in a *progression* toward a more complete picture. That is to say, what we find only hinted at in earlier texts will be fleshed out by the time we arrive at that culminating treatise on eschatology—the book of Revelation. You may be surprised at the limited number of texts that address the person of the

Antichrist and wonder if it justifies the mountains of paper and ink devoted to the subject!

Glimpses from the Old Testament

First the Old Testament source texts.

The Little Horn

Several passages in the book of Daniel describe visions of fantastic creatures; others appear to refer to historical personages from the intertestamental period. In both cases the texts also reach far into the future to a more ominous person. For this reason the following passages have been identified by biblical commentators throughout the ages as referring to the Antichrist.

The first is found in Daniel 7, where a "little horn" emerges from a ten-horned beast, the last of a series of four beasts that emerge from the sea:

> While I was thinking about the horns, there before me was another horn, a little one, which came up among them; and three of the first horns were uprooted before it. This horn had eyes like the eyes of a man and a mouth that spoke boastfully. . . .
> Then I continued to watch because of the boastful words the horn was speaking. I kept looking until the beast was slain and its body destroyed and thrown into the blazing fire.
>
> Daniel 7:8, 11

Here is an important clue to the character and work of the "little horn": He will speak arrogantly, making great, boastful declarations. But against whom—and why? The answer is found later in the same chapter:

> He will speak against the Most High and oppress his saints and try to change the set times and the laws. The saints will

be handed over to him for a time, times and half a time. But the court will sit, and his power will be taken away and completely destroyed forever.

verses 25–26

The little horn will speak arrogantly against the one true God. But since God is forever beyond his reach, this satanically inspired individual will unleash his wrath against the saints of the Most High. This reminds us of the words of Jesus to His disciples: "All men will hate you because of me" (Luke 21:17).

The text also indicates a set period of time during which the little horn—or Antichrist—will hold sway: "A time, times and half a time." If *time* here means *year*, as is commonly interpreted, then the Antichrist will persecute the saints for three and a half years.

Interestingly, here as in virtually every Bible passage referring to the Antichrist, we find the announcement of his certain defeat and destruction: "His power will be taken away and completely destroyed forever." The Bible leaves us with no doubts regarding the outcome of the final conflagration.

The King of Fierce Countenance

The second Old Testament passage referring to the Antichrist is Daniel 8, where Daniel describes his mysterious vision about a succession of four kingdoms that will follow from those of Media, Persia and Greece:

In the latter part of their reign, when rebels have become completely wicked, a stern-faced king, a master of intrigue, will arise. He will become very strong, but not by his own power. He will cause astounding devastation and will succeed in whatever he does. He will destroy the mighty men and the holy people. He will cause deceit to prosper, and he will consider himself superior. When they feel secure, he will

destroy many and take his stand against the Prince of princes.
Yet he will be destroyed, but not by human power.

Daniel 8:23–25

In the next verse Daniel is told that this vision "concerns the distant future." Once again we find the mention of the persecution of the saints as well as this king's contemptuous attitude. To this is added an allusion to his skill in deceit: He will be a "master of intrigue."

At long last he will challenge the "Prince of princes," a reference to the coming Messiah Jesus. From this we can infer that the Antichrist will proceed from a considerable power base, both political and military, more details of which will emerge later.

The Coming Prince

In the next chapter the angel Gabriel appears to Daniel in a vision in which he reveals a prophetic timetable of seventy groups of "sevens" (or years) leading up to the consummation of all things.

After the sixty-two "sevens," the Anointed One will be cut off and will have nothing. The people of the ruler who will come will destroy the city and the sanctuary. The end will come like a flood: War will continue until the end, and desolations have been decreed. He will confirm a covenant with many for one 'seven,' but in the middle of that 'seven' he will put an end to sacrifice and offering. And one who causes desolation will place abominations on a wing of the temple until the end that is decreed is poured out on him.

Daniel 9:26–27

We learn several things from this text: first, that the Anointed One will be "cut off." This was fulfilled at the crucifixion of Jesus Christ around A.D. 30. Following this is the destruction of "the city and the sanctuary." This was fulfilled in A.D. 70, at the culmination of the first Jewish revolt against Rome, when Jerusalem and the Temple were destroyed. This also fulfilled the words of Jesus: "I tell you the truth, not one stone here will be left on another; every one will be thrown down" (Matthew 24:2).

It was the Roman army under Titus that besieged and leveled Jerusalem. They are the "people" alluded to in Daniel 9. But note carefully what is said about those responsible for this infamous act in Jewish history: They are described as "the people *of the ruler who will come.*" But who is the "ruler who will come"? The rest of the passage makes clear that it is none other than the Antichrist.

Thus, if "the ruler who will come" is related to the "people" responsible for the destruction of Jerusalem, then we may surmise that the Antichrist will somehow arise out of the Roman empire. Here we have an important clue as to the origin of the Antichrist.

In this passage we also learn something of the program of the Antichrist. It is said that he "will confirm a covenant with many for one 'seven.'" *Seven* here is commonly taken to mean "a group of seven years." In the middle of that "week," however, he will break the covenant, or peace treaty. That the Jewish people are in view here seems clear by the reference to "[putting] an end to sacrifice and offering." This can only mean the Levitical Temple sacrifices— which tells us one more thing: The Temple will be rebuilt and sacrifices again be offered.

Sometime after the rebuilding of the Temple, the Antichrist will perform what is known as the "abomination of desolation." There is a historical precedent to this blasphemous act just prior to the Maccabean Revolt in 168 B.C. At that time the Seleucid ruler Antiochus Ephiphanes IV, as part of his drive to subjugate Judea by imposing Hellenistic religion and culture, desecrated the

Temple precincts. We do not know exactly what he did, but it is thought that Antiochus IV either sacrificed a pig on the altar of sacrifice or else erected a statue to Zeus in the Temple, or perhaps both. In either case, this provocative act was called by the Jewish historian Flavius Josephus the "abomination of desolation."

In Matthew 24:15 Jesus speaks about yet another abomination of desolation, this time committed by the future Antichrist. Just as Antiochus IV assumed the grandiose title *Ephiphanes,* meaning "God revealed," the Antichrist will also claim divine honors for himself. We can see this more clearly in the next passage.

The Willful King

Daniel 11 describes the political and military exploits of a series of "kings" identified by historians as the successors of the empire of Alexander the Great. These men ruled Syria and Egypt, and the last one mentioned in the text is Antiochus IV of Syria. The first 35 verses fit the historical record with such precision that Porphyry, the third-century A.D. Neo-Platonic philosopher and opponent of Christianity, contended that the text was a forgery.

According to Porphyry, it was written not by Daniel in the sixth century B.C. but by unknown authors in the second century *after* the events took place. Largely because of their denial of the possibility of supernatural prophecy, modern critical commentators have accepted the theory of an avowed enemy of the Christian faith.

After verse 35, however, the text diverges from the historical record as we know it and seems to project far into the future to describe one of whom Antiochus IV was only a pale shadow:

> The king will do as he pleases. He will exalt and magnify himself above every god and will say unheard-of things

against the God of gods. He will be successful until the time
of wrath is completed, for what has been determined must
take place. He will show no regard for the gods of his fathers
or for the one desired by women, nor will he regard any god,
but will exalt himself above them all.

Daniel 11:36–37

Here the reprobate character of the Antichrist is revealed in his monstrous self-exaltation above all other
gods. The mention that he will show no regard for "the
one desired by women" probably does not refer (as some
have supposed) to his sexual orientation.[1] Rather, it likely
refers to an ancient Jewish tradition that the deepest desire
of every Jewish woman was to be the bearer of the
promised Messiah. Thus we learn of the Antichrist's utter
enmity toward the eternal Son of God, Jesus Christ.

The passage goes on to describe the Antichrist's consummate political and military skills in creating his worldwide power base:

He will attack the mightiest fortresses with the help of a foreign god and will greatly honor those who acknowledge him.
He will make them rulers over many people and will dis-
tribute the land at a price.

Daniel 11:39

The text continues that the Antichrist will manage to
"invade many countries and sweep through them like a
flood" (11:40). One of the countries he will invade is "the
Beautiful Land," which refers to the land of Israel. But in
spite of his phenomenal success on the battlefield, forces are
being arrayed against him, and he is destined to be embroiled
in bloody conflicts leading to his eventual downfall:

But reports from the east and the north will alarm him, and
he will set out in a great rage to destroy and annihilate many.
He will pitch his royal tents between the seas at the beauti-

ful holy mountain. Yet he will come to his end, and no one
will help him.

Daniel 11:44–45

Conclusion

This brings to an end the principal Old Testament texts
that deal with the Antichrist. Let us draw together some
of what we have learned about him:

1. He will, in some fashion not explained in the text,
   be related to or arise out of the old Roman Empire.
2. He will possess unparalleled skills at intrigue, which
   will facilitate his meteoric rise to the pinnacle of
   world power.
3. The length of his rule will be limited to seven years.
   In the middle of that time there will be a decisive
   break in which he will repudiate his covenant with
   the Jewish people.
4. He will speak arrogant, blasphemous things against
   the most high God and—perhaps beginning at the
   midpoint of the "week"—will embark on a savage
   persecution of the saints.
5. He will conquer many countries militarily and at
   some point invade the land of Israel.
6. He will meet his end at the height of his power,
   despite phenomenal success against his enemies on
   the battlefield, through divine intervention.

Glimpses from the New Testament

Now let's turn our attention to the New Testament texts
that deal with the coming Antichrist. They enlarge on
these themes.

The Man of Sin

An important text in the New Testament yielding information about the Antichrist is found in 2 Thessalonians:

> He opposes and exalts himself over everything that is called God or is worshiped, and even sets himself up in God's temple, proclaiming himself to be God. . . . And then the lawless one will be revealed, whom the Lord Jesus will overthrow with the breath of his mouth and destroy by the splendor of his coming. The coming of the lawless one will be in accordance with the work of Satan displayed in all kinds of counterfeit miracles, signs and wonders, and in every sort of evil that deceives those who are perishing. They perish because they refused to love the truth and so be saved. For this reason God sends them a powerful delusion so that they will believe the lie and so that all will be condemned who have not believed the truth but have delighted in wickedness.
>
> 2 Thessalonians 2:4, 8–12

Here is another, more explicit reference to the "abomination of desolation"—his demand to be worshiped as God in a rebuilt Jewish Temple. In addition, we now learn of the Antichrist's ability to deceive mankind with "counterfeit miracles, signs and wonders." The source of these supernatural powers will be Satan himself.

In a sobering reference to "those who are perishing," the apostle Paul provides insight into why so many will fall for the delusions wrought by the Antichrist: because, tragically, "they refused to love the truth and so be saved." Yet this was not God's intention, for we read elsewhere, "He is patient with you, not wanting anyone to perish, but everyone to come to repentance" (2 Peter 3:9).

The Beast

Now we come to the book of Revelation, where we find the most in-depth discussion of the Antichrist to be found in Scripture. Yet even here the discussion is remarkable for its symbolism and sparseness of detail. The inspired writer paints his canvas with broad, vivid strokes. It has been left to the prophecy teachers to wrangle over the minutiae.

In chapter 13 we read about a beast with ten horns and seven heads coming out of the sea:

> The dragon gave the beast his power and his throne and great authority. One of the heads of the beast seemed to have had a fatal wound, but the fatal wound had been healed. The whole world was astonished and followed the beast. Men worshiped the dragon because he had given authority to the beast, and they also worshiped the beast and asked, "Who is like the beast? Who can make war against him?"
>
> The beast was given a mouth to utter proud words and blasphemies and to exercise his authority for forty-two months. He opened his mouth to blaspheme God, and to slander his name and his dwelling place and those who live in heaven. He was given power to make war against the saints and to conquer them. And he was given authority over every tribe, people, language and nation. All inhabitants of the earth will worship the beast—all whose names have not been written in the book of life belonging to the Lamb that was slain from the creation of the world.
>
> Revelation 13:2–8

The picture of the Antichrist in this passage, although shrouded in apocalyptic language, complements what is presented in previous texts. Again we see references to the beast receiving worship and blaspheming God. But here we find a curious new detail: The beast will suffer an apparently fatal wound but will somehow recover. This astounding turn of events merits two more allusions in the same chapter (verses 12 and 14) and later in the book of Revelation (17:8 and 11).

Prophecy buffs often surmise that this seeming resuscitation from the dead will be the catalyst to cement the Antichrist's worldwide following. But will it?

Commentators like the Bible teacher Dr. M. R. DeHaan took the position that a resurrected Judas Iscariot would be the future Antichrist. This view is based on similarities between the two: Both are called "the one doomed to destruction" (John 17:12; 2 Thessalonians 2:3). In referring to Judas, Jesus said: "Have I not chosen you, the Twelve? Yet one of you is a devil!" (John 6:70). Also, Judas is the only man other than the Antichrist whom it is said that "Satan entered" (Luke 22:3).

Most expositors, however, prefer not to identify the Antichrist with any deceased historical person brought back to life, for the simple reason that it grants Satan the power of resuscitation from the dead.

The text itself provides a clue as to the probable meaning of the passage, stating that "one of the heads of the beast *seemed* to have had a fatal wound" (italics mine). It is more likely that the deadly wound will be a clever subterfuge—one of the Antichrist's counterfeit miracles warned about in 2 Thessalonians 2:9. Another possibility is that the Antichrist will actually suffer a grievous wound that only seems to be fatal and from which he recovers.

Worldwide Rule?

It is commonly taught from Revelation 13 that the entire world will be under the sway of the Antichrist. Indeed, doesn't the text state that "he was given authority over every tribe, people, language and nation" (verse 7)?

A careful appraisal of the evidence, however, reveals a different picture. While it is undoubtedly true that the Antichrist will wield unprecedented worldwide power and influence, it will by no means be absolute. Daniel

11 states, "Many countries will fall, but Edom, Moab and the leaders of Ammon will be delivered from his hand" (verse 41). Neither will his rule go unchallenged. The text goes on to state that "reports from the east and the north will alarm him, and he will set out in a great rage. . ." (verse 44). Military forces are arraying themselves against the Antichrist; it is clear, near the end of his reign, that he has failed to consolidate his rule.

Moreover, even terms such as *all* and *the whole world* must be understood in context. While Revelation 13:3, for example, says, "The whole world was astonished and followed the beast," this cannot mean *everybody* because the Antichrist furiously persecutes those who refuse to worship him. Revelation 7 describes "a great multitude that no one could count, from every nation, tribe, people and language, standing before the throne and in front of the Lamb" (verse 9). Later the apostle John is told that they are those "who have come out of the great tribulation" (7:14). These are saints from every corner of the globe who have neither bowed the knee to the Antichrist nor taken his mark—at great cost.

The text goes on to describe a second beast, identified in Revelation 16:13 as the false prophet. Together with the great red dragon of chapter 12, symbolizing the devil, they constitute the ultimate perversion: a Satanic trinity. Here, in one of the most enigmatic passages of prophetic scripture, the second beast employs economic coercion to force mankind to worship the first beast, the Antichrist:

> Because of the signs he was given power to do on behalf of the first beast, he deceived the inhabitants of the earth. He ordered them to set up an image in honor of the beast who was wounded by the sword and yet lived. He was given power to give breath to the image of the first beast, so that it could speak and cause all who refused to worship the image

to be killed. He also forced everyone, small and great, rich and poor, free and slave, to receive a mark on his right hand or on his forehead, so that no one could buy or sell unless he had the mark, which is the name of the beast or the number of his name.

This calls for wisdom. If anyone has insight, let him calculate the number of the beast, for it is man's number. His number is 666.

Revelation 13:14–18

This passage has fueled endless speculation about the supposed worldwide powers of the Antichrist. On the basis of this and other passages we have already discussed, prophecy teacher J. R. Church paints an all-too-common picture of the Antichrist's rule:

> According to Daniel 7, the antichrist will rise to power during the days of a ten-nation confederation. He will be asked to aid a group of ten European nations, which together will attempt to establish a loosely-knit world government. There are three main areas he will seek to develop: a one-world monetary system, a one-world political system, and a one-world religion. Monetarily, he will convert all of the currencies of the world into one currency and will attempt to make it mandatory for all people to receive a mark in their right hand or in their forehead in order to be able to buy or sell.[2]

The idea of a one-world monetary system complete with a universal currency has been propagated with such assurance that many Bible students assume it is clearly taught in Scripture. Rather, the belief about a one-world monetary system is an *inference*—or, to put it another way, an *educated guess*—based on what little information is actually provided by the text.

Church goes on to describe the worldwide political rule of the Antichrist:

Politically, he will rise to power on the platform of peace. It is my opinion that the Battle of Gog and Magog will be the catalyst on which he rises to power. After the defeat of Russia, he will be hailed as the great peacemaker and will be considered to be *the savior of the human race.*

We have already seen that such phrases as *the whole world* do not mean everybody without exception. In fact, it seems there will be formidable military power blocks representing substantial areas of planet earth that are in rebellion against the Antichrist, as Church himself admits:

> Various governments will become disenchanted with the rule of the antichrist. In fact, it is my opinion that *the whole world will turn against the antichrist,* and will bring their armies against him and Israel.

Perhaps at this point you are musing, "Some world government!" No sooner are we told confidently that the Antichrist will be proclaimed "the savior of the human race" than we learn that "the whole world will turn against the Antichrist"—and all this in a remarkably short period of time. If so, it is not likely that those nations rising up against him will implement the so-called universal currency program of their enemy. With such concerted opposition, it is also difficult to see exactly in what sense the Antichrist is the political leader of the world.

What's going on here? The problem can be put simply: Too much is being read dogmatically into the biblical texts.

Rather than build an ultimately self-contradictory scenario, isn't it preferable to observe modesty and not go beyond what holy Scripture clearly states?

Field Marshal of Armageddon

The beast appears again in Revelation 16 as the world prepares for the greatest battle of human history:

> Then I saw three evil spirits that looked like frogs; they came out of the mouth of the dragon, out of the mouth of the beast and out of the mouth of the false prophet. They are spirits of demons performing miraculous signs, and they go out to the kings of the whole world, to gather them for the battle on the great day of God Almighty. . . .
> Then they gathered the kings together to the place that in Hebrew is called Armageddon.
>
> Revelation 16:13–14, 16

The satanic troika, in one supreme effort to defeat the host of heaven and ascend to the throne of God, will draw the armies of the world to Armageddon in the land of Israel. There is no room for doubt, however, as to the outcome of this decisive battle:

> They will make war against the Lamb, but the Lamb will overcome them because he is Lord of lords and King of kings—and with him will be his called, chosen and faithful followers.
>
> Revelation 17:14

Conclusion

How shall we summarize the above biblical texts? There seems little doubt that the Antichrist will be the most powerful political and military leader the world has ever known, and that large areas of the world—though by no means the whole world—will come under his control. He will inaugurate the greatest persecution against the saints that the world has ever witnessed. Toward the end of his remarkably brief rule, his political power base will disintegrate as he becomes embroiled in military con-

flict. The final battle will actually be waged against the
Lamb, the Lord Jesus Christ, and the Antichrist will meet
his end at the battle of Armageddon.

Given the tentative nature of the biblical texts, it is
remarkable that so many dogmatic ideas about the
Antichrist are abroad. But such speculation is not new;
Christians have sought to identify the Man of Sin since
the earliest days of the Church.

Interestingly, some historic theories about the Antichrist
sound more convincing than the current crop of candidates. We begin with an eccentric Roman emperor who
was the focus of speculation about the Antichrist for hundreds of years after his turbulent reign.

9

The Wandering Caesar

T he year was A.D. 68 and Rome was in turmoil. The enemies of Lucius Domitius Nero, the reigning Caesar for the last fourteen years, were finally gaining the upper hand. A momentous event in the Empire was about to take place that would haunt Christian apocalyptic thinking for hundreds of years. The man whose reign had begun so promisingly had degenerated into a wandering minstrel obsessed with grandiose illusions and incapable of governing the Empire.

Like his predecessor Claudius, Nero had ascended the throne by intrigue. His ruthlessly ambitious mother, Agrippina, had incestuously married her uncle, Claudius, after poisoning her husband. After eliminating all opposition among the palace advisors, Agrippina engineered her son's rise to power in A.D. 54 by poisoning Claudius, too.

In his first speech to the Senate, Nero promised a new Golden Age, and for the first five years of his reign exhibited generosity and moderation toward his subjects. Historians record a long list of laudable improvements in the political and social life of Rome, including an end to capital punishment and the bloody circuses.

Nero also exhibited a remarkable degree of toleration toward those who plotted against him. (Claudius, by contrast, had condemned some forty senators to death.) Nero cut taxes, granted new rights to slaves and promoted the theater and athletics as alternatives to the violent gladiator combats. He provided disaster relief to cities and even gave financial aid to the Jews at the request of the historian Flavius Josephus, the author of *Antiquities of the Jews* and *The Jewish Wars*.

But in A.D. 59 something snapped. Nero embarked upon a maniacal reign of terror that likely saw the deaths (among countless others) of the apostles Peter and Paul in Rome. The image of the infamous ruler that the name *Nero* conjures began to emerge, along with the reason people today name their sons Peter and Paul—and their dogs Nero. The same year he consented to the assassination of his increasingly insane mother, Agrippina, followed by that of his own wife, Octavia. The latter grim event was occasioned by his having fallen in love with the beautiful Poppaea Sabina, wife of the senator Otho. In time Poppaea also perished as a result of Nero's abuse.

The notorious fire that ravaged Rome for nine days in A.D. 64 consumed much of the city. Nero was blamed, though he was 35 miles away at the time at his villa at Antium. A strange religious sect called Christianity, newly established in the capital, was also blamed for starting the fire. The following year Nero put down a revolt with brutal force, resulting in the deaths of not only Seneca and the poet Lucan, but many others innocent of the conspiracy.

Oddly, parallel to the historical portrait of a brutal tyrant stands a lesser-known side of Nero: that of an aspiring poet, lyre player and theatrical performer. He was also deeply attracted to mystical religions at a time when not only the Jews but the Greeks, Romans and peoples of the East were awaiting a new god. He dabbled in Zoroastrianism, Gnosticism and perhaps even Christianity (as indicated by a fresco in the Palatine Chapel depicting Nero and the apostle Paul conversing).

At the end of A.D. 66, smitten by the Sirens' call from the land of the gods, Nero spent fifteen months wandering throughout Greece as a barefoot, long-haired ascetic, reciting poetry and playing his music. His obsession with the mystical religions of Greece when the Empire was reeling from revolts in Africa, Gaul and Spain, not to mention Judea, earned him the contempt of his fellow Romans. Nero, in blissful distraction, occupied himself with composing songs and inventing a hydraulic organ on which to play his music. He laughed at the growing threats to the Empire and popular discontent at home, claiming, "I have only to appear and sing to have peace once again in Gaul!"

The end was near. Condemned by the Senate to die a slave's death on the cross, abandoned by the Praetorian Guard, Nero fled the city. Arriving at one of his villas outside Rome, seeing that all hope was lost, Nero stabbed himself and was buried by his Christian mistress, Acte (according to his wishes), in a white sheet.

Would He Be Back?

Gone but not forgotten. Already before his death the Christians in Rome had called Nero the Antichrist for his vile actions and attempts to deify himself by enforcing emperor-worship. Now, the fact that he had died almost alone in an obscure place, passing from the scene without even a state funeral, gave rise to rumors that the minstrel emperor was not dead. Speculation abounded that he had somehow managed to escape east to the Parthians, the barbaric hordes who were the dreaded enemy of Rome. From there, it was said, he would one day return to wreak a fearsome revenge on the city that had turned against him.

These rumors, though unfounded, spread rapidly through the Empire and continued with amazing persistency into the next century and beyond. Decrees appeared allegedly from the hand of Nero. More ominously, Roman historians record no fewer than three instances in which impostors arose claiming to be Nero, one of whom convinced a large number of Parthians, throwing Achaia and Asia Minor into terror.[1]

The early Christians were influenced by these popular legends about Nero and many considered him the Antichrist. As time passed some thought he would rise from the dead to wage war against Rome. This apocalyptic battle would occur at the end of the age prior to the Second Coming of Jesus Christ. The apocalyptic *Ascension of Isaiah,* dated from the end of the first century, echoes this belief:

> And after it has been brought to completion, Beliar will descend, the great angel, the king of this world, which he has ruled ever since it existed. He will descend from his firmament in the form of a man, a king of iniquity, a murderer of his mother—this is the king of this world.[2]

The description of the Antichrist as "a murderer of his mother" is, of course, a reference to Nero's assassination of Agrippina in A.D. 59.

The legend of *Nero redivivus* (Nero resurrected) was held by Christian writers long after the first century. Jerome, writing at the end of the fourth century, affirmed that it was still held by many Christians even in his day.[3] One reason so many early Christians were convinced Nero was the Antichrist comes from a cryptic passage in the book of Revelation: "This calls for wisdom. If anyone has insight, let him calculate the number of the beast, for it is man's number. His number is 666" (Revelation 13:18).

The meaning of 666 has been the source of speculation throughout the centuries. Claims popularized in recent years that 666 refers to the Social Security number of the Antichrist or some futuristic computerized identification code fail to interpret the verse in its historical context. The modern mind may consider it strange to designate someone's name by a number, but those living at the end of the first century, when Revelation was written, would have understood the writer's intention.

The apostle John was in all likelihood employing the use of *Gematria*, the practice of discovering hidden meaning in a word by computing its numerical value. This method of interpreting words and texts is well-attested in the ancient world of the Hebrews and Greeks.

The languages of both the Jews and the Greeks, which used the letters of the alphabet to denote numbers, lent themselves to the practice of Gematria. Some early Christian documents, for example, use *888* for the name of Jesus in Greek. Graffiti on the excavated walls of Pompeii provide further illustration of the common practice of assigning numerical values to names. Also, the Jewish rabbis sought hidden meaning in the Old Testament through the use of Gematria.[4]

Accordingly, the attempts of the early Church to decipher the meaning of 666 focused on the numerical value of the names of possible Antichrist candidates. But, as you can imagine, an amazing number of names can be doctored through the use of variant spellings and substituting letters to yield 666.

The early Church Father Irenaeus records several possibilities in the Greek language but seems not to have considered any in the Hebrew language. The book of Revelation, however, was written by the apostle John, a Jew from Galilee. Even though the text of Revelation was written in Greek, the *lingua franca* of the Roman world, John would have been more familiar with Hebrew Gematria than its Greek counterpart. So it is not surprising to discover that the Hebrew transliteration of the Greek for *Caesar Nero* adds up to the required 666. This is fascinating for another reason, too—but before I give it, we must retreat a few paces and note that in some manuscript traditions Revelation 13:18 reads *616* instead of *666.*

This has always presented a thorny problem for commentators. Irenaeus, for example, mentions that many in the second century held to the 616 reading. Some proposed solutions such as *Caesar Gaius* (Caligula) were based on 616 rather than 666. It is significant to note that when Nero's name is written according to its Latin form, you get the number 616. Thus we have a possible explanation for the variant reading that developed in some manuscript traditions. That is to say, as the Latin language came into general use, the text may have been altered from 666 to 616 by well-meaning copyists.

So here is the other reason it is interesting that the Hebrew transliteration of the Greek for *Caesar Nero* adds up to the required 666: John's use of his native Hebrew Gematria may help clarify his statement that wisdom and insight are necessary to decipher the number of the beast. There were doubtless many converted Jews among the

Christians of the churches of Asia Minor to whom Revelation was addressed. This may also explain why, elsewhere in the text of Revelation, John makes special mention of the Hebrew form of certain names.[5]

Does all this mean the apostle John believed Nero was the Antichrist (implying an error on the part of the inspired writer)? More likely John was pointing his readers cryptically to Nero as a type or forerunner of the coming Antichrist, who exhibited many of the characteristics of the future beast of Revelation.[6]

In fact, the belief that a historical figure could prefigure the future Antichrist was widely held by the early Church Fathers:

> Tertullian was the first of the patristic writers to pick up this idea from John and to suggest that any current heretic or rebel against Christ is Antichrist. He also taught that this rebellious spirit would be personified in the Antichrist who will appear at the end of time. Cyprian and Origen followed this idea. Origen declared that the principle of the Antichrist has had or will continue to have many proponents during the course of history. . . . Not only will the Antichrist appear at the end of time, but his spirit is now embodied in all the enemies of Christ.[7]

Connections with the Antichrist

How did Nero manage to earn such enduring association with the coming Antichrist? Let's review two major characteristics of his rule that bear resemblance to the coming Man of Sin:

1. The first several years of Nero's reign, in which he instituted many commendable reforms, were laudable. Within a comparatively short period of time, however, Nero's personality underwent a dramatic transformation

and his regime turned despotic. The early Church historian Eusebius records this change:

> When Nero's power was not firmly established he gave him-
> self up to unholy practices and took up arms against the God
> of the universe. To describe the monster of depravity that he
> became lies outside the scope of the present work. Many
> writers have recorded the facts about him in minute detail,
> enabling anyone who wishes to get a complete picture of his
> perverse and extraordinary madness, which led him to the
> senseless destruction of innumerable lives, and drove him in
> the end to such a lust for blood that he did not spare even
> his nearest and dearest but employed a variety of means to
> do away with mother, brothers, and wife alike, to say noth-
> ing of countless other members of his family, as if they were
> personal and public enemies. All this left one crime still to
> be added to his account—he was the first of the enemies to
> be the declared enemy of the worship of the Almighty God.[8]

For many early Christians this brought to mind the
future king described as a "master of intrigue" by the
prophet Daniel:

> He will become very strong, but not by his own power. He
> will cause astounding devastation and will succeed in what-
> ever he does. He will destroy the mighty men and the holy
> people. He will cause deceit to prosper, and he will consider
> himself superior.
>
> Daniel 8:24–25

As the first persecutor of the Christian Church, Nero
indeed attempted to destroy "the holy people" as recorded
by Tertullian:

> Study your records: there you will find that Nero was the
> first to persecute this teaching [Christianity] when, after sub-
> jugating the entire east, in Rome especially he treated every-

one with savagery. That such a man was author of our chastisement fills us with pride. For anyone who knows him can understand that anything not supremely good would never have been condemned by Nero.[9]

The statement that "in Rome especially he treated everyone with savagery" after conquering the East is likely a reference to the persecution of Christians. This event took place in A.D. 64 when Nero's armies defeated the Parthians. In the same year Rome was burned, for which the Christians were blamed.

2. Most ancient commentators dwell on the fact that Nero put his wife and mother, along with other family members, to death. He also exhibited contempt for traditional Roman gods and attempted to install the cult of the Syrian virgin-mother goddess Atargatis in Rome. This reminded Christians of the prediction in Daniel: "He will show no regard for the gods of his fathers" (11:37, NASB).

Nero's obsession with Eastern religions led him to rebuild the city of Rome in Greek style after it was ravaged by the great fire. The centerpiece of the reconstructed city was the fabulous "Golden House," which was consecrated to Nero's new gods and goddesses. It was the most ambitious building ever designed for Rome. Had it been completed, the complex would have covered a full third of the city.

As for the reference to self-deification, such honors were part of the Roman civil cult and customarily awarded to the emperor by the Senate on his death. The story is told of the mortally ill emperor who, in a moment of lucidity, exclaimed: "I feel that I am about to become a god!" In Nero's case, however, the usual magnificent state funeral and accompanying divine honors were denied him.

The centuries would come and go; the *Nero redivivus* legend would fade along with the last vestiges of the

Roman Empire. It would not be until the end of the eighteenth century that a brilliantly successful and charismatic ruler would arise on the European continent who, it appeared, might be the fulfillment of the biblical Antichrist.

10

The King of France

L et's face it, most present-day Antichrist candidates appear bland compared to those of former days when Christians had reason to believe they were living in the very last days. Those were the days when potential Antichrists were real leaders, not Eastern-mystical wimps or pin-striped politicians who never led a battle charge in their lives. They were heads of empires, military leaders, men who knew how to conquer and rule.

Imagine the following scenario: An immensely charismatic and powerful European monarch extends his domain by military force to include much of the former Roman Empire. His army marches on Rome itself, the eternal city, bringing the Pope into his sphere of influence with a peace treaty. Next comes the Middle East; he occupies Egypt by force. But our conqueror's eyes are set on the Holy Land. Marching up the coastline at the head of a powerful army, he invades the ancient land of

Israel. Few oppose him, except—"ships of Tarshish" that harass his forces as he prepares for a decisive battle at Acco.

His army encamps at the very mouth of the plain of Megiddo, the traditional location of the prophetic battle of Armageddon. He journeys to the ancient site of the same name overlooking that expansive valley. Looking down from the summit, he observes that the setting is an ideal site for a battle of cataclysmic proportions. Meanwhile, powerful forces to the east and north prepare for battle against him.

Sound like Armageddon? You bet, and if it were happening today this leader would with one grand gesture sweep aside the other so-called Antichrist possibilities touted by various prophecy teachers. The problem is, this scenario played itself out two hundred years ago, and the man we are speaking about is, of course, Napoleon Bonaparte.

Gog Revealed . . .

The parallels between the greatest imperial dictator of European history and the biblical description of the Antichrist are uncanny. For starters, Napoleon was very nearly an Italian subject, bringing to mind the biblical passages linking the Antichrist with the revived Roman Empire. His mother tongue was a dialect of Italian. His place of origin, Corsica, was an island off the Italian mainland, the language and culture of which were closely allied with Italy. Fifteen months prior to Napoleon's birth, Corsica was deeded to France.

After a military education and commission as an artillery officer, Napoleon was promoted to brigadier general after distinguishing himself in a critical battle against anti-revolutionary forces at Toulon. Even so, his career faltered and he was reduced at one point to wandering the streets of Paris at half-pension and without an assignment.

As destiny would have it, a fresh opportunity presented itself when Napoleon was called on for assistance during an uprising in Paris in 1795. He demonstrated strategic genius and decisiveness in suppressing the revolt, and was rewarded by being appointed commander of the French occupation army of Italy.

The next few years brought dazzling success in a campaign against the Austrians fought on Italian soil. While the defeated Habsburgs sued for peace, Napoleon turned his attention toward southern Italy. In an epic campaign his army overcame all resistance on the Italian peninsula—including, significantly, his occupation of the papal states.

Napoleon's conquest of the Vatican territories and the vicar of Rome excited the imagination of students of Bible prophecy, as noted by historian Ernest R. Sandeen:

As the unbelievable events of the 1790's unfolded, students of . . . apocalyptic literature became convinced (in a rare display of unanimity) that they were witnessing the fulfillment of the prophecies of Daniel 7 and Revelation 13. The Revolution brought the cheering sight of the destruction of papal power in France, the confiscation of church property, and eventually the establishment of a religion of reason; the final act occurred in 1798 when French troops under Berthier marched on Rome, established a republic, and sent the pope into banishment. Commentators were quick to point out that this "deadly wound" received by the papacy had been explicitly described and dated in Revelation 13. Although prophetic scholars had previously been unable to agree on what dates to assign to the rise and fall of papal power, it now became clear, after the fact, that the papacy had come to power in 538 A.D.[1]

A.D. 538 plus 1260 day-years (the "forty-two months" of the beast's rule in Revelation 13:5) did indeed add up to 1798. As students of biblical prophecy cast a wary eye on the seemingly undefeatable French general, unfolding events seemed to mirror biblical prophecies down to the last detail.

Napoleon's next move read like a page out of the book of Daniel. With Austria vanquished and Italy subdued, Britain alone remained at war against France. Given England's mastery of the sea through its powerful navy under the command of Admiral Horatio Nelson, Napoleon realized that a cross-channel invasion would be folly. Forced to look for another way to bring the Anglo-Saxon foe of France to her knees, he conceived the daring plan of invading Egypt. This would both threaten England's vital trade route with India and encourage the *rajahs* (native rulers) to revolt against British rule.

Accordingly in 1798 he sailed with his army for Egypt, managing to elude Nelson's overwhelmingly superior fleet. After defeating the Mameluke army in the shadow of the great pyramids, all opposition collapsed and his army of 38,000 troops easily won control of the country. Events transpired rapidly. Admiral Nelson, who had been combing the Mediterranean in search of his prey, caught up with the French fleet at the Egyptian port of Abu Qir. All but two of the 55 French war vessels were destroyed in what came to be known as the Battle of the Nile, leaving Napoleon and his army stranded in Egypt.

Two unexpected developments now came into play: First, the Egyptian populace, whom Napoleon hoped would embrace him for liberating them from Turkish rule, revolted against their new conquerors. Then, in September 1798, Turkey declared war on France. Napoleon, anxious by now to quit Egypt, was forced to march up the coast into Palestine to secure the ports of Jaffa and Acre against the Turkish navy.

Students of biblical prophecy were perched on the edges of their seats, as Sandeen notes:

> The identification of the events of the 1790's with those prophesied in Daniel 7 and Revelation 13 provided biblical commentators with a prophetic Rosetta stone. At last a key had been found with which to crack the code. There could now be general agreement upon one fixed point of correlation between prophecy and history. After 1799, in Egyptology as in prophecy, it seemed as though there were no limits to the possibility of discovery.[2]

The primary event of 1799 in relation to biblical prophecy was Napoleon's invasion of the Holy Land, which seemed at the time to be an uncanny fulfillment of Daniel 11:

> At the time of the end the king of the South will engage him in battle, and the king of the North will storm out against him with chariots and cavalry and a great fleet of ships. He will invade many countries and sweep through them like a flood. He will also invade the Beautiful Land. . . . Egypt will not escape. He will gain control of the treasures of gold and silver and all the riches of Egypt, with the Libyans and Nubians in submission. But reports from the east and the north will alarm him, and he will set out in a great rage to destroy and annihilate many.
>
> Daniel 11:40–44

Surely no military conqueror in all of European history could "invade many countries and sweep through them" like Napoleon. And who but Napoleon had managed to "gain control of the treasures" of Egypt? Like the Antichrist of Daniel 11, he was "alarmed" by reports from "the east and the north," which in relation to his position in Egypt seemed to describe the Turkish forces. Lastly, the reference to the "king of the North" coming against him with "a great fleet of ships" sounded precisely like the Turkish attack on Napoleon's army, despite its defeat in a second battle at Abu Qir by French forces.

Napoleon and his army, as it turned out, managed to occupy Jaffa but ground to a halt north of Mount Carmel at Acre, which withstood his siege with help from the British fleet offshore. And here a verse from Ezekiel's prophecy concerning Gog of the land of Magog came into play:

> You will say, "I will invade a land of unwalled villages; I will attack a peaceful and unsuspecting people—all of them living without walls and without gates and bars." . . . [But] Sheba and Dedan and the merchants of Tarshish and all her villages will say to you, "Have you come to plunder? Have you gathered your hordes to loot, to carry off silver and gold, to take away livestock and goods and to seize much plunder?"
>
> Ezekiel 38:11, 13

The Hebrew word here translated "villages" can also mean "young lions," and appears as such in the King James Version, which was in wide use among Protestants at the turn of the nineteenth century. The connection was made immediately with the British Empire, whose national symbol was also the lion!

Tarshish was an ancient maritime power whose colonies extended to faraway coastlines—perhaps, it was thought, to the shores of Great Britain itself. This interpretation found further support from a verse in Daniel: "Ships of the western coastlands will oppose him, and he will lose heart" (Daniel 11:30).

And so we have it: Gog—identified as Napoleon—was successfully opposed at the siege of Acre by the "lion," or the naval fleet of Great Britain. Napoleon turned back and eventually escaped from Egypt, leaving behind his army, which was doomed to capitulation. The similarity to the prophetic texts proved remarkable, and there was more to come.

... And the Beast

Napoleon showed little interest in Christianity personally. But, realizing the truth of Voltaire's dictum that the common man needs religion, he signed a Concordat with the Pope in 1801 recognizing Roman Catholicism as the majority religion of France. Protestant churchmen were quick to find parallels with Revelation 17:

> There I saw a woman sitting on a scarlet beast that was covered with blasphemous names and had seven heads and ten horns. . . . This title was written on her forehead:
>
> MYSTERY
> BABYLON THE GREAT
> THE MOTHER OF PROSTITUTES
> AND OF THE ABOMINATIONS OF THE EARTH.
>
> I saw that the woman was drunk with the blood of the saints, the blood of those who bore testimony to Jesus.
>
> Revelation 17:3, 5–6

Since the time of the Reformation many Protestants had identified the Pope as the Antichrist. Here, in a new twist, Roman Catholicism became the great harlot of Revelation 17, while Napoleon himself was the "beast," or Antichrist, on whose back the harlot rode—a fitting description, for early nineteenth-century Christians on both sides of the Atlantic, of the Concordat between Napoleon and the Pope. Both would use the other for their own nefarious purposes.

If that did not seal the identification of Napoleon as the Antichrist, the military campaigns against England, Austria and Russia that followed would remove any lingering doubt from the minds of many prophecy-watchers. These were renowned battles on land and sea that live in the minds of schoolchildren in Britain and France. There were epic victories for England at Trafalgar in 1805, and for France at Austerlitz later the same year.

It was France's great Slavic foe, however, that above all excited the imaginations of students of Bible prophecy. Around this time George Stanley Faber published two studies that reflected current speculation regarding events on the Continent.[3] Faber identified Napoleon as the Antichrist, who as head of a revived Roman Empire would once again invade the Middle East. But his ambitions would once again be thwarted by "the ships of Tarshish" (Isaiah 60:9), which Faber (like other loyal British subjects) identified as England. Faber saw the Ottoman Turks as "the kings from the East" of Revelation 16:12, who would also join the battle of Armageddon soon to be fought in the Holy Land. Russia, according to Faber, was "the king of the North" of Daniel 11:40 destined to engage the Antichrist in battle.

Thus were the pieces of the eschatological puzzle now in place and awaiting the final countdown. The Antichrist (Napoleon), at the head of a revived Roman Empire, had invaded the Holy Land once; it was rumored that he planned to do so again. Arrayed against him were forces from the east (Turkey) and the north (Russia), who would also play their parts in this unfolding drama.

But it was not to be. Napoleon had fought Russian forces earlier at Austerlitz and again in 1807. But the disastrous invasion of Russia in 1812 reduced Napoleon's *grande armee* of a half-million men to about twenty thousand soldiers still in formation. The Russian defeat would herald the beginning of the end of his rule. Back in France rumors were flying that Napoleon had been killed in battle, and a rival general nearly succeeded in a *coup d'état* before Napoleon hastened back to Paris.

Curiously, despite his failure on the Russian front, this incident appeared to fulfill yet another cryptic biblical reference to the beast, which "seemed to have had a fatal wound, but the fatal wound had been healed" (Revelation 13:3). The fires of prophetic speculation were stoked once again.

By 1815, however, the prophetic scenario built up around Napoleon was on the verge of collapse. When Napoleon met the British and Dutch forces under the command of the Duke of Wellington at Waterloo, the beleaguered emperor of France was nearly a spent man. Shortly afterward he abdicated for the last time and was sent into exile. Another possible Antichrist had failed to live up to the grand expectations of prophecy enthusiasts.

As candidates for the position of Antichrist go, Napoleon Bonaparte's credentials would make most contemporary prophecy teachers drool. But he was not the Antichrist. It would not be for another century, when Europe was racked with political upheaval, that a far lesser ruler would become the focus of prophetic speculation.

11

The Fettuccine Fascist

In the midst of the two cataclysmic World Wars that engulfed the world in the first half of the twentieth century, a political and military leader emerged on the European continent who occupied the attention of prophecy teachers and their followers for more than a decade. Attention was focused (contrary to what we might expect) not on Adolf Hitler but on his Axis fellow dictator to the south, Benito Mussolini.

In the aftermath of World War I the borders of the European continent had been redrawn. Bible students were closely watching political developments on the continent for signs of the "revived Roman Empire" that they saw predicted in Bible prophecy. One of those tentative new nations was Italy, which emerged from the war beset by economic and social instability. Out of the tumult rose ex-schoolteacher Benito Mussolini, who preached a fiery brand of nationalism and promised the revival of the Italian empire.

Prophecy watchers in America could hardly believe their ears—and it was coming straight out of Rome itself. A closer parallel to the Antichrist's revived Roman empire could scarcely be imagined. All eyes were on "Il Duce."

Mussolini was appointed premier in 1922. Two years later, following a rigged election won by terrorizing the opposition, the Fascists finally obtained a majority in the Italian cabinet. Mussolini promptly dissolved all rival political parties and inaugurated a one-party state.

While many American prophecy teachers were sizing up the new Italian dictator as a possible Antichrist, others, impressed by Il Duce's fervent anti-Communism, saw him in a different light. Arno C. Gaebelein, respected Bible teacher and editor of the prophecy monthly *Our Hope*, referred to "Mussolini's good and helpful work." Gaebelein noted that "the fascist leader always carried a NT and was friendly towards Protestant missions and schools in Italy."[1]

This naïve assessment did not wash for very long. Besides the fact that Mussolini was a lifelong atheist and author of anticleric novels, other evidence was fast accumulating that seemed to link the Italian Fascist with the beast of Revelation. After all, wasn't an egotistical, bombastic leader uttering "proud words and blasphemies" (Revelation 13:5) destined to arise out of Rome, the capital city of the Antichrist? Furthermore, with the signing of the Lateran Treaty and the Concordat of 1929, Mussolini was effectively joining forces with the Roman Catholic Church, considered by many to be the citadel of apostate Christendom.

The Pentecostal Evangel showed great interest in these developments. Noting that Bible students had long awaited the predicted revival of the Roman Empire, the magazine pointed the finger at the dynamic Italian leader as a likely fulfillment of biblical prophecy. One writer suggested that Mussolini would join forces with the "one-world" organization of that day—the League of Nations:

> Why, therefore, should it be thought incredible that a revived Roman Empire may be in the process of formation as another link in the wonderful chain of events of the last days? May it not be that Mussolini's dream will affect the future of the present League of Nations? Who can tell? The one thing that would give power to the League would be the presence of a strong personality who would force himself by circumstances to its leadership; or a new Roman combine of nations may draw to itself those destined to form part of that confederacy which will for a time dominate Europe and wield the despotic power of the Antichrist.[2]

The above-quoted words, with names, nations and organizations interchanged, would constitute a recurrent prophetic theme in the decades to come—indeed, right up to the present day.

In the same year, 1926, Oswald J. Smith, pastor of People's Church, Toronto, presented evidence that the Antichrist would make his appearance within two years. He based his bold statement on a series of purported prophecies given by a Rabbi Michael in 1868, including the prophecy of a great war in 1913, which Smith took to be close enough to the start of World War I. More significant in Smith's eyes was the rabbi's prediction of the complete redemption of Israel by 1928, a date confirmed by other students of prophecy.[3]

Emboldened by the seemingly inescapable turn of events, Smith wrote a tract in 1926 entitled "Is the Antichrist at Hand?" In it he voiced the view that the times of the Gentiles—the period of Gentile domination of world affairs spoken of by Jesus in Luke 21:24—had begun in 604 B.C. at the captivity of Jerusalem by Nebuchadnezzar. Smith calculated that the times of the Gentiles would last 2,520 years, ending in 1917. This date was in itself significant as the year that the Balfour Declaration, which expressed the intention of the British government to establish a national homeland for the Jewish people, had been signed.

But the year 1917 had passed. Undeterred, Smith set to work recalculating the times of the Gentiles, this time taking as his starting point the final fall of Jerusalem, which he (virtually alone among scholars) dated at 588 B.C. That yielded a termination date for the times of the Gentiles of 1933—just seven years away from 1926. The significance of this new date was not lost on Smith:

> If our chronology is correct it means that all these things, including the great tribulation, the revival of the Roman empire, the reign of Antichrist, and the battle of Armageddon must take place before the year 1933.[4]

Smith was not alone in his identification of Benito Mussolini as the Antichrist. Noted preacher and Bible teacher Harry A. Ironside pulled out all the stops in his description of the Italian dictator:

> His bombastic utterances backed up by tremendous ability to perform have astonished the world. He declares himself the Man of Destiny, chosen to revive the Roman Empire and restore it to its pristine glory. The Mediterranean, he declares, shall yet become a Roman lake surrounded by nations in alliance with Italy. His grandiose plans move on to fulfillment in spite of all opposition. At least six powers are in alliance with Italy, and that the remaining ones will join the confederation seems to be just a question of time.[5]

One can readily imagine the persuasive effects of these words, penned during the early decades of this century, on the hearts and minds of prophecy students. Many contemporary enthusiasts are excited about far lesser candidates who either hold purely symbolic positions of honor in the royal houses of Europe or else have no political base whatsoever. Mussolini, by contrast, was a ruler installed in Rome, thought to be the seat of the "ten-nation confederacy" led by the Antichrist. In addition, he commanded (albeit badly) the military forces of a nation. With the prophetic time clock to all appearances running down, two Belgian prophecy teachers well known in American circles, Mr. and Mrs. Ralph Norton, resolved to clinch the journalistic scoop of the century and perhaps for the entire Church age: an interview with the potential Antichrist himself. Traveling to the very seat of power of the suspected beast of Revelation, they unabashedly attempted to pin him down with leading questions, as reported later in several American Christian magazines:

> During their meeting with Mussolini, they asked him if he intended to rebuild the Roman Empire. He answered that it would be impossible. "We can only revive its spirit, and be governed by the same discipline." Evidently the Nortons were not satisfied with his answer, so they informed him of the biblical prophecy about the new Roman Empire of the last days. According to the Norton's report, "Mussolini leaned back in his chair and listened fascinated, and asked, 'Is that really described in the Bible? Where is it found?'"[6]

Il Duce must have disappointed his questioners by his apparent ignorance of the role he was supposed to be fulfilling. With hindsight the whole adventure seems a little far-fetched. You can imagine future potential Antichrists being interrogated by enterprising prophecy teachers anxious to announce what has judiciously remained hidden in sacred Scripture.

Mussolini's invasion of Ethiopia in October 1935 caused a mixed reaction among American prophecy enthusiasts. On the one hand, it did constitute a downward thrust into a region bordering the Middle East. Also, Ethiopia is indeed mentioned as an ally of Gog in Ezekiel 38 (*Cush* in the NIV). In the end, however, Mussolini's inept bungling as the Italian supreme commander in one military campaign after another eventually disqualified him for consideration. Moreover, prophecy teachers had arrived at the remarkable conclusion that "Mussolini was too egotistical, blunt, and undiplomatic" to be the Antichrist of the last days.[7]

By the time Mussolini was unceremoniously shot by Italian partisans in 1945, the "revived Roman Empire" of his bombastic rhetoric had crumbled before the advancing Allied forces. Another nominee for the position of Antichrist, this one conveniently from the eternal city itself, had failed to live up to expectations.

Other possibilities have since been proposed, including one who apparently chooses to remain behind the scenes.

12

The Lord of East End

The story of one of the most widely publicized Antichrist candidates ever to join the field managed to captivate the attention of prophecy-watchers and New Agers alike. And although he has declined so far to make his much-awaited appearance, few took notice that the whole affair had the marks of a world-class hoax.

Prophecy teachers, in their haste to reveal the Man of Sin, were by no means least to take note of the grandiose claims uttered by the personable, smooth-talking Scot who served as publicist for "Lord Maitreya." To top off what turned out to be a grand exercise in gullibility, this story comes complete with some mystifying twists.

First the story.

On Sunday, April 25, 1982, readers of the *New York Times* opened their newspapers to discover an unusual full-page advertisement proclaiming:

The World Has Had Enough . . . Of Hunger, Injustice, War.
In Answer To Our Call For Help, As World Teacher For All
Humanity,
> THE CHRIST IS NOW HERE

The paid advertisement, which appeared in major newspapers around the world, was sponsored by an esoteric organization called The Tara Press located in London. Tara Centers were said to exist in North Hollywood, New York City and 125 other cities in the U.S. and Canada. The ad campaign was organized by a magnetic personality, Benjamin Creme, a 58-year-old artist from Scotland who described himself as a disciple of Lord Maitreya.

The advertisement continued to describe the soon coming of "the Christ":

> How Will We Recognize Him?
> Look for a modern man concerned with modern problems—political, economic, and social. Since July 1977, the Christ has been emerging as a spokesman for a group or community in a well-known country. He is not a religious leader, but an educator in the broadest sense of the word—pointing the way out of our present crisis. We will recognize Him by His extraordinary spiritual potency, the universality of His viewpoint, and His love for all humanity. He comes not to judge, but to aid and inspire.

The advertisement then asks, "Who is the Christ?"

> Throughout history, humanity's evolution has been guided by a group of enlightened men, the Masters of Wisdom. They have remained largely in the remote desert and mountain places of earth, working mainly through their disciples who live openly in the world. This message of the Christ's reappearance has been given primarily by such a disciple trained for his task for over 20 years. At the center of this 'Spiritual

Hierarchy' stands the World Teacher, Lord Maitreya, known by Christians as the Christ. And as Christians await the Second Coming, so the Jews await the Messiah, the Buddhists the fifth Buddha, the Muslims the Imam Mahdi, and the Hindus await Krishna. These are all names for one individual. His presence in the world guarantees there will be no third World War.

The reference to a cadre of enlightened men called "the Masters of Wisdom" who are secretly guiding the spiritual development of humanity is a recurrent theme of Eastern-occult thought. But why must the message—and, indeed, the teacher himself—remain concealed from the common man?

The answer lies in the doctrine of reincarnation, which permeates all Eastern religions and occultism. Reincarnation rejects the view that all men are created equal. Rather, humans are classed according to their "spiritual enlightenment"—an endeavor that has resulted in the gross injustices of India's caste system. Only the privileged few who are "sufficiently enlightened" have the right to be exposed to the hidden teachings of the Masters.

The reference to these so-called Masters hidden in "remote desert and mountain places" may be an oblique reference to the Hindu gurus and Tibetan lamas found in remote regions of India and the Himalayas. But claims about divine figures waiting in obscure places to be revealed recalls Jesus' warning concerning false Christs:

> So if anyone tells you, "There he is, out in the desert," do not go out; or, "Here he is, in the inner rooms," do not believe it.
>
> Matthew 24:26

Why are we not to believe such claims? Because, as the next verse describes, there will be no mistaking the glorious appearance of Jesus Christ:

> For as the lightning comes from the east and flashes to the west, so will be the coming of the Son of Man. Wherever there is a carcass, there the vultures will gather.
> Immediately after the distress of those days "the sun will be darkened, and the moon will not give its light; the stars will fall from the sky, and the heavenly bodies will be shaken." At that time the sign of the Son of Man will appear in the sky, and all the nations of the earth will mourn. They will see the Son of Man coming on the clouds of the sky, with power and great glory.
>
> Matthew 24:27–30

Regardless of when Jesus returns, this much is certain: He promised to return "on the clouds of the sky, with power and great glory." On that day there will be no doubt in anyone's mind what has happened. So Maitreya, along with every other self-described "Christ," has already failed the acid test.

But for now there is still time to deceive the multitudes. The advertisement continues, offering a sampling from the teachings of Maitreya:

> ### What Is He Saying?
> "My task will be to show you how to live together peacefully as brothers. This is simpler than you imagine, My friends, for it requires only the acceptance of sharing.
> "How can you be content with the modes within which you now live: when millions starve and die in squalor; when the rich parade their wealth before the poor; when each man is his neighbor's enemy; when no man trusts his brother?
> "Allow Me to show you the way forward into a simpler life where no man lacks; where no two days are alike; where the Joy of Brotherhood manifests through all men.

"Take your brother's need as the measure for your action and solve the problems of the world."

There is doubtless much with which men and women of good will can agree regarding these words of Maitreya. After all, shouldn't we be striving for the elimination of hunger, poverty and strife? Jesus warned, however, that in the last days men with great powers of deception will arise: "False Christs and false prophets will appear and perform great signs and miracles to deceive even the elect—if that were possible" (Matthew 24:24).

It is exactly such a "great sign" that the advertisement then promised:

> When Will We See Him?
> He has not as yet declared His true status, and His location is known to only a very few disciples. One of these has announced that soon the Christ will acknowledge His identity and within the next two months will speak to humanity through a worldwide television and radio broadcast. His message will be heard inwardly, telepathically, by all people in their own language. From that time, with His help, we will build a new world.

What Happened?

The end of two months fast approached with no sign of Maitreya. The Tara Center newsletter *Emergence* dated June 10, 1982, described the course of action of the New York City Tara Center's increasingly bewildered staff.

Under the direction of Benjamin Creme, who was in turn guided by his psychic contacts, some thirty devotees of the center flew to London in a desperate bid to locate the promised Christ before the deadline expired. They fanned out across East London in hopes of locating Maitreya by following Creme's instructions. After contacting the police, newspapers and various community agencies in a fruitless attempt to find their Christ, Tara Center devotees were reduced to asking strangers if they had ever heard of such a person. The newsletter describes their dogged efforts:

> As nightfall approached, Ben's master directed us to an increasingly specific location where we might find the meeting. By 8 o'clock there were nearly 30 of us colorfully dressed pilgrims, wandering the otherwise deserted streets in a nondescript section of London. We found no one except each other.

Needless to say, the devotees of the New York City Tara Center were so disillusioned that they subsequently suspended publication of their newsletter. The mastermind behind the Maitreya campaign, however, was not to be deterred.

Benjamin Creme had first received a telepathic message from his spiritual "master" in 1959, said to be a member of a council of advanced spiritual beings known as the Hierarchy. Creme was led to believe he would play a vital role in the soon return of the Christ. Sometime after 1975 Creme claims he began receiving telepathic communications from Maitreya, although he had not yet met him in person. These communications typically voiced concern for the problems of the planet for which he, Lord Maitreya, had the solution.

Let's notice, before we continue with our story, that this deceptive aspect of the Antichrist—as being a great humanitarian and the benefactor of the human race—was foreseen by Christians from early times, as evidenced by this fourth-century description of the Antichrist by Saint Ephrem:

> To conciliate many he plots craftily that he may be loved
>   soon by the peoples

Neither gifts shall he accept nor speak in anger
He shows himself not sullen but ever cheerful
And in all these well-planned schemes
He beguileth the world so long as he shall rule
For when the many peoples and nations shall behold such
        great virtues—fair deeds and powers
All of one mind shall become
And with great joy shall crown him
Saying one to another—Surely there is not found
Such [another] man—so good and just.[1]

Much attention has been focused on the negative side of the Man of Sin—his diabolical character, the war he wages throughout the world, his relentless persecution of the saints. At the outset of his career, however, he will present himself as the consummate man of peace. Benjamin Creme has portrayed his "Christ" in the same benevolent terms, as a man of great compassion for the poor and suffering.

But Christians know Maitreya is not the Christ. Nor can he be, according to the terms Jesus Himself laid out, because the Second Coming will be an unmistakable event. And if Maitreya is not the true Christ, then he is an impostor, which means that the source behind Maitreya must be the evil one—the liar, deceiver and destroyer about whom Jesus warned His disciples:

> He was a murderer from the beginning, not holding to the truth, for there is no truth in him. When he lies, he speaks his native language, for he is a liar and the father of lies. Yet because I tell the truth, you do not believe me!
>
> John 8:44–45

Whom are jittery non-Christians to believe as we approach the turn of the millennium: the "masters" guiding Benjamin Creme concerning the alleged Christ

Maitreya (who remarked offhandedly that the last time
he came he was called Jesus, the Christ), or Jesus Christ
Himself, the Son of God, who promised to come again
on the clouds of the sky with great glory? They cannot
both be right.

Notwithstanding the attempt to identify Maitreya with
Jesus Christ, the soon-to-be-revealed "Christ" and his
spokesman Benjamin Creme display a startling arrogance
toward the faith at which Jesus is the heart. In an interview that appeared in the March 21, 1982, edition of *The
Denver Post*, Creme asserted that Maitreya was in fact
superior to Jesus of Nazareth, who was but his lowly disciple. According to the reporter:

> . . . [Creme] explained that by The Christ he means not Jesus
> Christ, but the Master of Wisdom of whom Jesus and such
> other spiritual leaders as Mohammed, Brahma and Krishna
> are disciples.

Creme then stated that after Maitreya makes his debut
to a waiting world, all existing religions will be swept
aside and work will begin toward laying the groundwork
for "a single global religion." The reporter posed the obvious question:

> "Won't the advent of a single world religion annoy the hier-
> archies of all the current orthodox religions?" I asked. "More
> than that," he said with a smile. "They will be shocked. I
> daresay they will be among the last to accept the new age."
> But, he said confidently, it will come anyway, because it must.
> "We will begin to live," he said, ". . . as potential gods."

This last statement betrays what Creme actually means
by *they*. Though he does not single out Christians for cen-
sure, it is clear they are his target. It is not, after all, the
religions of Brahma or Krishna that refuse to accept the

equality of humanity with God. That "heresy" can be laid squarely at the feet of monotheistic biblical faith. In the pages of the Bible, the only suggestion that man can become gods comes from the enemy of the true God— none other than Satan himself. Disguised as a serpent, he offered the supreme temptation:

> The woman said to the serpent, "We may eat fruit from the trees in the garden, but God did say, 'You must not eat fruit from the tree that is in the middle of the garden, and you must not touch it, or you will die.'" "You will not surely die," the serpent said to the woman. "For God knows that when you eat of it your eyes will be opened, and you will be like God, knowing good and evil."
>
> Genesis 3:2–5

The belief that all men are essentially gods (though some are more divine than others) constitutes the cornerstone of Eastern-occult (these days called New Age) thought. It is only the Judeo-Christian worldview as revealed in the Bible that stands in opposition to this satanic notion, proclaiming the one true God separate from His creation. This is why Christianity and Judaism, of all the religions and philosophies of the world, remain the focus of attack. We minimize or seek to avoid this raging spiritual battle at our own peril.

Creme predicted confidently that out of the "decomposed church" will arise the new metaphysical teaching of the divine oneness of all humanity. He added, in an oblique reference to the Bible, that "we do not need scriptures to experience our true Selves."

During one of the times Creme served as a medium for the alleged spirit messages of his master, Maitreya allegedly spoke the following:

> My Friends, My children, I am here to show you that there exists for Man a most marvelous future.

Decked in all the colours of the rainbow, glowing with
the light of God, Man, one day, will stand upright in His
Divinity. . . .

May this manifestation lead you to seek and to know that
Self which is God. . . .

Manifest around you that which I pronounce and become
as Gods.[2]

Throughout the 1980s Benjamin Creme continued his
efforts to prepare mankind for the coming of Maitreya
and to enlist the support of the media. He summoned
news conferences at which he encouraged those present
to make a joint declaration that Maitreya would "welcome an opportunity to address all mankind through the
linked TV channels in a way that will convince the world
of his true status."

While journalists balked at being used in such a manipulative fashion, prophecy teachers jumped into the fray,
touting Maitreya as the possible Antichrist. In *Prophecy
in the News* J. R. Church ran a series of articles high-
lighting Maitreya, the first of which concluded with this
admonition: "If [Creme's] Lord Maitreya is that final
antichrist, then prepare for the rapture!"[3]

Constance Cumby warned solemnly: "Maitreya is living somewhere. He eats. He sleeps. He paces the floor.
He studies world conditions. He knows his time is
soon."[4]

Meanwhile, Creme tapped the evidently well-heeled
Tara Center for the funds to sponsor another full-page
advertisement, this one in the January 12, 1987, issue of
USA Today. It promised that Maitreya alone held the
solution to the problems of drugs, AIDS, poverty, crime,
starvation, terrorism and the nuclear threat. In another
reference to the inherent divinity of all human beings, the
advertisement stated that "the solution lies within YOUR
grasp." As to when we would see him, the ad quoted

Maitreya himself: "It is My intention to reveal myself at the earliest possible moment, and to come before the world as your Friend and Teacher."

A Child from the East

Maitreya did not reveal himself as expected, and we might be tempted to relegate this strange figure to the ash heap of failed Antichrist candidates. But I promised some unique twists to this story, and for them we must leave Maitreya for a moment and journey back to the early 1960s.

Compared to the current explosion of Eastern mysticism and occultism and the thinning moral and spiritual fabric of our society, it was an age of innocence. It was still possible in those days to maintain that, in the words of Rudyard Kipling, "East is East and West is West." The onslaught of Hindu gurus flooding to the West would not begin in earnest until the late '60s, along with the growing prominence of occultists such as Anton LaVay and his Church of Satan. That left the comparatively tame psychics and crystal ball readers as the main practitioners of occultism in the U.S.—an outlandish fringe ignored by most of American society.

One of these clairvoyants and newspaper prognosticators, Jeane Dixon, amused journalists at the end of every December with her predictions for the coming year. Mrs. Dixon hardly constituted a credible threat to the influence of Christianity in American society, but one detailed and mysterious prediction caught the attention of those interested in biblical prophecy. This "revelation," as described in her book *My Life and Prophecies,*[5] is set in ancient Egypt and revolves around a child of royal Egyptian birth. The infant is no ordinary child:

> But my eyes were drawn to Nefertiti and the child she tenderly cradled in her other arm. It was a newborn babe,

wrapped in soiled, ragged swaddling clothes. He was in stark contrast to the magnificently arrayed royal couple. Not a sound broke the unearthly silence as they issued forth with the child. I then became aware of a multitude of people that appeared between the child and me. It seemed as though the entire world was watching the royal couple present the baby. Watching the baby over their heads, I witnessed Nefertiti hand the child to the people. Instantly rays of sunlight burst forth from the little boy, carefully blending themselves with the brilliance of the sun, blotting out everything but him.

page 183

The child's father, Pharaoh Ikhnaton, disappeared from the scene and Nefertiti was stabbed in the back and died. The child grew and appeared at first to be a Christ figure:

My eyes once again focused on the baby. By now he had grown to manhood, and a small cross which had formed above his head enlarged and expanded until it covered the earth in all directions. Simultaneously, suffering people, of all races, knelt in worshipful adoration, lifting their arms and offering their hearts to the man. For a fleeting moment I felt as though I were one of them, but the channel that emanated from him was not of the Holy Trinity. I knew within my heart that this revelation was to signify the beginning of wisdom, but whose wisdom and for whom? An overpowering feeling of love surrounded me, but the look I had seen in the man when he was a babe—a look of serene wisdom and knowledge—made me sense that here was something God allowed me to see without my becoming a part of it. I also sensed that I was once again safe within the protective arms of my Creator.

page 183

In an earlier book, *The Gift of Prophecy*, Dixon presented what she called the "child from the East" in a positive light. In this book, however, she apparently had a change of heart and came to believe he will lead many astray:

What does this revelation signify? I am convinced that this revelation indicates a child, born somewhere in the Middle East shortly after 7:00 A.M. on February 5, 1962—possibly a direct descendant of the royal line of Pharaoh Ikhnaton and Queen Nefertiti—will revolutionize the world. There is no doubt that he will fuse multitudes into one all-embracing doctrine. He will form a new "Christianity," based on his "almighty power," but leading man in a direction far removed from the teachings and life of Christ, the Son.

page 184

Later Dixon stated that "there is no doubt in my mind that the 'child' is the actual person of the Antichrist, the one who will deceive the world in Satan's name" (p. 194). Her vision of this "Antichrist" being worshiped by the people of the world brings to mind the beast of Revelation:

> Then I saw another beast, coming out of the earth. He had two horns like a lamb, but he spoke like a dragon. He exercised all the authority of the first beast on his behalf, and made the earth and its inhabitants worship the first beast, whose fatal wound had been healed.
>
> Revelation 13:11–12

This raises a puzzling question for which I have no ready answer: Why would a practicing occultist like Jeane Dixon experience a "revelation" *warning* about the Antichrist? One would expect those who engage in practices contrary to the Bible to *welcome* a vision of the Antichrist.

The Identity of Maitreya

And what does this cryptic prophecy of Jeane Dixon have to do with Maitreya? The connection came in 1991 with the appearance of a book written by an alleged former employee of Creme's Tara Center. The author, writing under the pseudonym Troy Lawrence, claimed to have infiltrated "one of the nerve centers of New Age activity." His book, purporting to unveil the "secret plans spawned by the occult hierarchy," was promoted on the jacket as the culmination of "years of undercover investigation, late-night clandestine meetings and disguised rendezvous with New Age elite."[6]

Lawrence claims to have taken considerable personal risk in coming forth with his revelations:

> "I've placed my life in danger to get this information out," says Lawrence. "We all know what has happened to some who have come out of the New Age movement and tried to tell their story. . . . People must read this book before it's too late!"[7]

Lawrence's book, entitled *New Age Messiah Identified*, rekindled interest in Maitreya among prophecy teachers. The book claims to have uncovered the identity of this mysterious so-called "Christ." Maitreya's given name, according to Lawrence, is Rahmat Ahmad, a Pakistani living in London. Ahmad is the nephew of Khalifat-ul-Masih IV, the leader of the militantly anti-Christian Ahmadiyyah Movement headquartered in Rabway, Pakistan. As his uncle's designated successor, Ahmad is the heir to the title Khalifat-ul-Masih V, fifth in line after the movement's founder, Mirza Ghulam Ahmad.

Ghulam Ahmad was born in India in the latter part of the nineteenth century and was fervently opposed as a young man to the efforts of Christian missionaries to convert Hindus and Muslims. Ghulam, of Muslim background, devoted himself to the refutation of these missionaries. At some point (perhaps under the influence of Helena Blavatsky's occult Theosophical Society, which was also campaigning against missionaries in India at the time) Ghulam was apparently possessed by the "masters."

His contacts with these spiritual beings convinced him he was the promised Messiah figure predicted by many religions. Ghulam claimed to be the reincarnation of the Hindu Krishna and Gautama Buddha, the Imam Mahdi of Islam, the Jewish Messiah and the Second Coming of Jesus Christ all rolled into one.

Even though Ghulam presented himself as the fulfillment of the eschatological expectations of all religions, his writings demonstrate that he never swerved from his primary objective, the refutation of Christianity. Prophecy teacher J. R. Church lent support to Lawrence's allegations by quoting Ghulam:

> The mischief of this age proceeds from Christian priestcraft and the object is to break the Cross. Therefore I have been sent in the guise of Jesus to fulfill the prophecy which is generally known as the second advent. . . . Those people are grievously at fault who think that Jesus is still alive in the heavens. . . . The mischief of Christians has exceeded all limits. The vile abuse and extreme insult that their learned men have, by pen and tongue, poured out upon [the] Holy Prophet has caused a ferment in the heavens.[8]

In order to "break the Cross" and convince Christians that Jesus was dead, Ghulam propagated the ancient fiction that Jesus did not die but recovered after being taken down from the cross. He later traveled to Kashmir in search of the lost tribes of Israel where, according to Ghulam, He died and was buried. To this day Ahmadiyyah missions around the world propagate this myth aggressively, producing literature containing photographs of the purported tomb of Jesus in northern India.

According to Troy Lawrence, the great-great grandson of Ghulam Ahmad, Rahmat Ahmad, lives among the Ahmadiyyah community in southeast London. Although personal information about Rahmat is said to be closely guarded, he has reportedly studied at Oxford University and often gives lectures before Ahmadiyyah and New Age groups.

Lawrence, if he is to be believed, discloses one other curious piece of information about Maitreya—and here is the tie-in with Jeane Dixon's prophecy about the Antichrist. Although the exact day of his birth is not known, Lawrence claims that Rahmat Ahmad was born in February 1962, the very month in which Jeane Dixon had her startling "revelation" about the Antichrist.[9]

A Case of Mistaken Identity

The fact that Rahmat Ahmad (alias Maitreya) was allegedly born in the same month as Jeane Dixon's Antichrist child is a potentially fascinating piece of information. But I was nagged by a question: Was Lawrence to be believed?

Some things on the face of it did not add up. Rahmat and Dixon's Antichrist do not match in every detail. Pakistan, for example, is not considered part of the Middle East. Nor is there any known evidence that Rahmat is of Egyptian descent and possibly a direct descendant of Pharaoh Ikhnaton, as in Jeane Dixon's vision.

Another difficulty: The beast of Revelation is portrayed as a political and military leader; whereas the religious leader of a relatively small Muslim sect is unlikely to be in a position to wield such power. This problem was once illustrated in another context by the Soviet leader Josef Stalin who, when informed that the vicar of Rome opposed his policies, remarked: "The Pope? How many divisions does he have?" I had to question how many divisions someone like Maitreya could hope to field.

Prophecy teachers, when they portray various religious leaders as the Antichrist, sidestep this difficulty by predicting that they will be catapulted to the highest reaches of political power when their time comes. To me it seems more likely that the Antichrist will have a formidable political power base already in place, which will then be expanded to worldwide proportions.

Since authors employing pseudonyms do not publish their addresses and telephone numbers, I had no recourse but to call the publisher. It did not take long for me to get the impression that inquiries about Troy Lawrence and *The New Age Messiah Identified* were not welcome. In fact, I was made to feel like a private eye poking around where I had no business. Not only did the receptionist refuse to respond to my questions, but she refused to transfer me to anyone else.

"That book was only in print a few months," she told me.

"Why was that?" I asked.

There was a pause. Finally she said, "I don't have any information about that."[10]

And the conversation was over.

I knew that a publisher would not dump the entire inventory of a new book for no reason. But because the name of a distributor appeared in the front of the book, plastered over that of the original publisher, I surmised that the remaining stock of books had been sold off. Maybe the distributor would answer some of my questions.

This time I had mixed success. The man in the front office seemed ignorant at first of any controversy surrounding *New Age Messiah*. No, he knew nothing about Troy Lawrence. But he did know someone who knew him personally. My hopes soared. I was instructed to call back later.

When I did, the man was more hesitant to talk with me. He had spoken with his contact, whom he described as "a totally impeccable source." This person had assured him that "Troy Lawrence," though using a pseudonym, was exactly who he said he was. A number of other people, also unidentified, could confirm what Lawrence said in his book.

"Then why do you think the publisher dropped the book like a hot potato?" I asked.

"Ah," he said. "There was one regrettable incident when Lawrence appeared on a television program. A man from the audience, someone who had a personal vendetta against him, challenged him, calling him a liar. Lawrence lost his cool and walked out."

Interesting—but enough reason for the publisher to drop the book?

There was one more item: The man at the distributor had been given something written by Lawrence to pass along to me. A minute later I had the fax in my hand. It was an article purportedly written by Lawrence after *New Age Messiah* had been published.

In it he claims that some of the fears expressed in the book have indeed come to pass:

> My life has been threatened many times. I have been physically attacked, and I've even been the victim of a high-speed chase—all in the hopes of silencing me. I have, however, never regretted my decision to go public, not even after I learned that a fellow laborer had been mysteriously killed.[11]

High-speed chases and mysterious deaths? Now I *was* beginning to feel like a private eye! What was Lawrence talking about? Then I remembered: Another author from the same publisher had indeed died under what were called "unexplained circumstances" shortly after completing a promotional tour for his book. The author, Randall Baer, had a story remarkably similar to Lawrence's. He, like Lawrence, was a former "New Age insider" who defected after becoming a Christian, then went public with his exposé of the New Age movement. His book was entitled *Inside the New Age Nightmare.*

My head was buzzing. Could Lawrence be telling the truth? Was it possible that he and other former New Agers were actually being hunted down? I wanted to find out more but had only one thin thread of a contact.

Repressing my normally reserved nature, I phoned back the man at the distributor. It proved unfruitful. He had said all he intended to say. I tried to find out where the information he had faxed me had come from. No dice. Indeed, he said he was under obligation to say nothing else.

Obligation to whom? Dark, mysterious worlds loomed ominously like thunderclouds. What was going on here, that seemingly harmless questions posed such a threat to whomever this man was in contact with?

But my detective work seemed to have come up against a brick wall—until I had a conversation with cult researcher Erik Pement of *Cornerstone* magazine. I was finally able to put a name to the shadowy pseudonym: It seems that Troy Lawrence's real name is Darrick T. Evenson. Moreover, it seems that Evenson is, to put it mildly, a theologically confused individual who has on various occasions claimed to be a Mormon, a Mason, a Jehovah's Witness and a New Ager.[12]

When I heard this, questions raced through my mind: Why did a well-known Christian publisher print the dramatic allegations of someone whose credibility had been compromised? How is it that a prominent prophecy ministry saw fit to give repeated sensational exposure to Evenson's story without corroborating it? Finally, and perhaps most baffling, why are apparently well-meaning individuals continuing to stand by someone who has ostensibly been exposed as a fraud?

It was not the first time. I remembered the notorious John Todd of the late 1970s, who inflamed considerable interest with his (as it turned out) bogus claims of involvement with the Illuminati. More recently, Mike Warnke of *Satan Seller* fame has also been exposed as having fabricated his story of involvement in Satanism and the Illuminati.

It seems difficult to avoid the conclusion that, when it comes to the subject of biblical prophecy, sensationalism sells. All this reinforces the importance of our using the discernment the Holy Spirit gives us to sort faction from fiction—regarding, for example, the identity of the Antichrist. As a general rule, until solid evidence is forthcoming, *we do well to consider all prophetic tidbits, no matter how fascinating, as speculation.*

A Cast of Thousands

If Maitreya should elect one day to make his appearance, one thing is certain: He will have to wait in line. A host of other names are currently being touted by various prophecy teachers, some of whom cultivate a veritable stable of "possibles."

One such individual worthy of mention is King Juan Carlos of Spain, whose name was advanced by the late Charles R. Taylor. Taylor strayed beyond what would be considered prudent by asserting dogmatically, with no qualification, that Juan Carlos *is* the Antichrist:

> In 1993, the signs are so overwhelming that King Juan Carlos I of Spain is the man who is soon to be appointed, acclaimed or crowned king, or even Emperor of the Western European revised and revived Roman Empire and become, therefore, the Antichrist of the Tribulation period, that I must present for your enlightenment and assurance

"the preponderance of the evidence" that this statement is verifiably true.[13]

The case Taylor makes in his book *The Antichrist King—Juan Carlos* is built almost entirely on the fact that Juan Carlos can trace his lineage to the Habsburg dynasty of Austria, which in turn arose out of the old Holy Roman Empire that governed Europe during the Middle Ages. This is the "evidence" that Juan Carlos is the king who will rule over the revived Roman Empire in the form of the European Economic Union.

Taylor neglected to mention that a considerable number of Europe's royal families claim a connection with the Habsburgs through intermarriage. It was the thing to do; there is nothing special in this regard about Juan Carlos.

Taylor presented Juan Carlos as a reigning king ready to take the reins of power in Europe. Not so. Juan Carlos is the titular head of Spain; he no more governs the Iberian peninsula than the Queen of England governs Great Britain. The government of Spain is in the hands of a democratically elected prime minister and his cabinet.

Much is made of insignificant events such as Juan Carlos' birthplace in Rome, his visit to the Holy Land and the fact that one of his obscure titles is *King of Jerusalem*.

In short, Taylor's book *The Antichrist King—Juan Carlos* is, to put it kindly, lacking in substance.

It is all the more surprising, then, to see respected prophecy teacher Jack Van Impe enthusiastically endorse Taylor's "phenomenal new book," which he describes as "scrupulously" and "painstakingly" researched:

> This person meets all the requirements set forth in God's Word. This person stands at the exact point where every prophecy about the Antichrist converges. . . . This book looks at the lone individual on the face of the earth today who meets every requirement, fits every descriptive detail, and

holds all the potential to become the Antichrist King: Juan Carlos, King of Spain.[14]

But by now we are used to all this. And hence the purpose of our abbreviated snapshot journey through the history of speculation about the Antichrist.

Let there be no question: I cast not the slightest doubt on the certainty of the Second Coming of Jesus Christ or on the reality of the upcoming Man of Sin. The presence of impostors and counterfeits merely confirms the existence of the original. But those impostors and counterfeits give us a sense of perspective from which to evaluate present-day claims about various Antichrist candidates.

Now let us turn to the heart of this book: We should not allow ourselves to become obsessed with the time of Jesus' return. A far more vital question needs to be addressed honestly by each of us: Are we ready to meet our Lord?

I look back on times when I was intensely interested in matters of biblical prophecy and the Second Coming; yet, to my shame, if I had been asked if I was truly prepared, I would not always have been able to give an unqualified "Yes!" All my fervor for biblical prophecy was therefore of little profit, for I had neglected the most important thing.

I trust, dear friend, that each one of us will joyfully anticipate, without shame, the glorious appearing of the Lord Jesus. Let's discuss how we can do this.

Part 3

How Shall We Then Live?

13

Just a Footstep Away

The breathtaking incident I am about to share is not an exaggerated story passed along and embellished with each telling. It was related to me by a close friend of the woman involved. The friend lived a few houses down the narrow lane from my wife, Rebekka, and me in Beit Jala near Bethlehem. While visiting her one day, Rebekka and I sat on her living room couch sipping strong Arabic tea as she unfolded a story almost too fantastic to believe. I will let you decide for yourself what to think of it.

Several years ago the city of Tacoma, Washington, was (like the rest of the state) living in dread of a shadowy serial killer to whom several grisly murders had been attributed. No one knew when or where the murderer would strike next, except for one trademark. He was called "the I–5 killer": Most of his victims were found near the interstate that ran the length of the state from the Canadian border on down through Portland.

The woman in this account, whom we shall call Marge, was a Christian housewife and mother who lived in a suburb near the I–5 expressway. One morning she was going about her normal routine, which for this particular day included ironing the wash. Marge was alone in the house—or so she thought. Suddenly she had a strong impression to go upstairs and read her Bible.

Now Marge, as our friend in Beit Jala described her, is a down-to-earth person definitely not given to dreams and visions. That is why this sudden sense struck her as so peculiar.

Marge's first reaction was to hold off until she finished the load of laundry. Then she would be free to have a special quiet time. It was silly to leave a hot iron and the rest of the clothes sitting on the table.

Then it came to her again: *Go upstairs and read your Bible—now!*

The impression was so strong that even though it seemed irrational, she knew immediately it had to be the Lord and that she had to obey. Without the vaguest sense of why she was interrupting her chores, Marge propped the iron at the head of the ironing board and headed upstairs to her bedroom. She went into the room and, without thinking, closed the door behind her.

She started to cross the room to where her Bible lay on the night table. Then another impression came: *Lock the bedroom door.*

This was all very confusing. Marge had never had an impression quite like this. But once again, sensing it was from the Lord, she obeyed. Retracing her steps, she locked the bedroom door and started back toward her nightstand. Then she heard it, and it sent a shock wave of terror through her.

The doorknob was turning. Someone was trying to open the door.

Providentially there was a phone in the bedroom. Marge rushed over, dialed the operator and asked frantically for the police.

Whether the intruder heard Marge call for the police or whether something else drove him away, he vanished.

But he did not go far. A short time later on the same day, a woman on the very next street was murdered, the latest victim of the I–5 killer.

This shocking account raised a sobering question with Rebekka and me as we talked with our friend in Beit Jala, and it raises a question for us in this book: Why was Marge spared what in all probability would have been an unspeakable tragedy? And why are other people subjected not only to physical evil but also (as we have abundantly seen) to spiritual evil?

To answer this question would require many learned volumes. Even then we would not plumb the depths of the unsearchable purposes of God. But we have gleaned some insights from our investigation into the phenomena of angels, aliens and the Antichrist.

To begin, let's return to the unfathomable world of alien abductions and examine the case of a woman who was *not* spared repeated demonic intrusions into her life. We now turn to the troubling case of Betty Andreasson.

"You Are Our Chosen One"

I tend to assume, along with many Christians, that we are immune to being "taken captive" in any sense of the word by evil spiritual entities. But the experience of Betty Andreasson forces me to reexamine what a person means who says he or she "professes faith in Jesus Christ."

That is what is puzzling about Mrs. Andreasson: She claims forthrightly to be a Christian, has attended evangelical churches, signs her letters *In Christ Jesus* and was once abducted while she was reading her Bible. Raymond

E. Fowler, who has chronicled her story over the past two decades, refers to her as a "devout Christian." Even Whitley Strieber professes admiration for Andreasson's "deep and exceptionally beautiful Christian faith," although he hastens to add that "it is far more pure than the twisted remnant that passes for modern fundamentalism."[1]

To find out what Strieber means, and to attempt to discover why some people are subjected to spiritual evil, we must examine what are purported to be the unusual occurrences of Betty Andreasson's life.

Wife and busy mother of seven children, Betty Andreasson is the last person you would expect to suffer abduction by aliens. Before the evening of January 25, 1967, the Andreassons lived what seemed to be a normal life in the small town of South Ashburnham, Massachusetts.

Betty was working in the kitchen that night about 6:35 P.M. when the walls of her ordinary existence came crashing down. As she tells it, first the lights of the house blinked off; then a pulsating, reddish-orange light shone through the kitchen window. Betty and her father, who had come into the kitchen when the power shut off, saw a group of small, strange beings approaching the house. Not waiting to be invited in, they passed right through the door. The creatures, five of them, stood between four and five feet tall and resembled one of the types of aliens familiar to abduction researchers.

According to Betty's account, the rest of her family were placed in some kind of suspended animation while Betty was spirited away to a small UFO craft that had landed in their backyard. Inside she was subjected to an unpleasant physical examination and taken to another place where she underwent "a painful yet ecstatic religiouslike experience."[2] Several hours later, at 10:40 P.M., Betty was returned home to find the rest of her family still in a trancelike state. They were all put to bed and the aliens left.

As is typical, the family remembered little of the experience. But with the passage of time, details began to emerge from Betty's own subconscious. Several years later she found herself responding to a story in the local newspaper about astronomer and noted UFO researcher Dr. J. Allen Hynek.

After her case came to Hynek's attention, Betty was subjected to a rigorous background check and her story was examined by a team of researchers that included a psychiatrist, solar physicist, aerospace engineer, telecommunications specialist and professional hypnotist. During a twelve-month investigation that included two lie detector tests, a psychiatric interview and fourteen hypnotic regression sessions, the investigators concluded that Betty Andreasson was a reliable witness and was not fabricating her experience.

As her story unfolded under hypnotic regression, the researchers learned that, as with so many abductees, the incident in 1967 was not Betty's first abduction. Nor would it be her last; the unearthly experiences would continue for more than twenty years.

The intervening years have brought Betty Andreasson little of the peace and few of the answers that the aliens have promised her repeatedly. Various homes in which she has lived have been dogged by poltergeist activity, as she and her family have endured disquieting sounds and strange apparitions that have kept their nerves on edge.

More disturbing are the abductions themselves, during which Andreasson has purportedly undergone painful and highly intrusive "examinations," the purpose of which she is not told. On one occasion her eye was removed and a long needle inserted into her brain. Another time tubes were inserted through her navel deep into her

body. A long, flexible needle was inserted up her nose to
retrieve a strange BB-shaped object that had been
implanted in her brain years earlier. These guinea pig-type
experiments seem to serve no other purpose than to engen-
der confusion and extreme fright in Andreasson. And all
along she is assured that she has been chosen to be the
spokeswoman for the aliens, who want to impart a vitally
important message to mankind.

During one abduction Andreasson heard a loud voice
stating, "I have chosen you."

She asked the voice if it was God and received an evasive reply: "I shall show you as time goes by."

This was not a satisfactory answer for Andreasson.
Afraid of deception, she defensively proclaimed her Christian faith, crying out, "There is nothing that can make
me fear. I have faith in Jesus Christ!"[3]

But the aliens, significantly, were able to calm her fears
by reassuring her with a shrewd reference to "the son,"
which Andreasson took to mean Jesus. As Fowler
describes it:

> "We know, child," the voice answered. "We know, child,
> that you do. That is why you have been chosen. I am send-
> ing you back now. . . . I can release you, but you must release
> yourself of that fear through my son."
>
> The words "through my son" suddenly became the cata-
> lyst for the most moving religious experience I have ever wit-
> nessed. Betty's face literally shone with unrestrained joy as
> tears streamed down her beaming face:
>
> "Oh, praise God, praise God, praise God. [Crying] Thank
> you, Lord. [Crying, sobbing] I know, I know I am not wor-
> thy. Thank you for your Son. [Uncontrollable sobbing]
> Thank you for your Son."[4]

It is important to note that evil spirits, during "channeling" (speaking through a medium), sometimes talk

about a metaphysical "cosmic Christ" and even mention the name *Jesus*. But they steadfastly refuse to confess the Lord Jesus Christ as God and Savior. Since Andreasson never received an answer to her question about God, and since she was apparently mollified by the vague reference to "the son," it seems clear that she was indeed being deceived by the "aliens."

Despite her stated belief that UFOs are God's angels, Andreasson apparently remained confused about what the aliens were and whom they served. Years later, in 1973, she still exhibited profound fright at the onset of a particular abduction experience.

It was night, and once again strange lights shone through the window. Andreasson's terror increased when she was unable to wake her husband. The outside lights were bright, and she knew they were coming for her. Under hypnotic regression guided by hypnotist Fred Max, she relived her fear:

> *Betty:* . . . And I'm covering my head with the covers. Whatever that is—Go away! Go away! Lord Jesus! Lord Jesus! Make it go away. Whatever it is, Lord Jesus. [breathing heavily] Oooooooo! Oooooooo!
> *Fred:* [almost whispers] Take it easy.
> *Betty:* Something's in the bedroom and it's pulling my arm! Oh! Oh! . . . Oh, I'm scared!
> *Fred:* Is it pulling you hard?
> *Betty:* It's pinching on my left arm, sorta. [Breathing heavily] Something's pulling the covers off my head. . . .[5]

As the bed covers were pulled off, Andreasson discovered several aliens in her bedroom. Another horrifying abduction experience had begun.

Why were her pleadings to the Lord Jesus for help ineffectual? On another occasion several years later, when Andreasson feared that the aliens were coming for her, she again called on the name of the Lord. This time not only were her appeals futile, but shortly afterward two of her sons were tragically killed in an automobile accident. This shattered Andreasson, who had been told repeatedly by her alien abductors that she was "blessed" and that they were watching over her life.

At last word Andreasson still has not resolved the question of the nature of the aliens and clings to her belief that they are the modern equivalent of biblical angels. In Raymond Fowler's 1991 book, *The Watchers: The Secret Design Behind UFO Abduction,* she asked him for his opinion. Fowler assured her there is nothing to fear from the aliens:

> Sometimes changes in traditional thought are distasteful and alarming to the generation in which they occur. However, [the aliens] in no way changed the basic message of the Christian Gospel in which you have faith.[6]

Fowler is correct, at least, in raising the key question of whether the aliens have altered the message of the Gospel. This is indeed the litmus test for anyone who claims to have the answers to mankind's problems. Unfortunately, Fowler is mistaken in his belief that the aliens—which Betty Andreasson prefers to call "angels"—do not present another Gospel. In none of her reported experiences with aliens do they confess the Gospel of Jesus Christ as presented in the New Testament. Instead they use religious terms—cleverly, obviously intending to deceive those with a certain acquaintance with the Bible and Christianity.

It is evident that many so-called angels, as well as UFO aliens and the coming Antichrist, are satanic counterfeits, deceivers of the first order who will lead vast numbers of men and women astray.

When Betty tells the voice that she has faith in Jesus Christ, she is told:

That is why you have been chosen. . . . I would never harm you. It is your fear that you draw to your body that causes you to feel these things. I can release you but you must release yourself of that fear through My Son.[7]

Betty is receiving a cynical reply from a voice pretending to be God the Father and informing her that she alone, not her abductors, is to blame for her lingering fears. Under hypnotic regression she recalls a theological discourse given to her during the same abduction by an alien named Quazgaa:

They have come to help the human race. . . . And unless man will accept, he will not be saved. He will not live. All things have been planned. Love is the greatest of all. . . . It is through the spirit but men will not search out that portion. . . . Within the highest of the high and the lowest of the low are many answers. Man will find them through the spirit. Man is not made of just flesh and blood. . . . The knowledge is sought out through the spirit and those that are worthy are given. Those that are pure of heart, that seek with earnestness, will be given.[8]

This typical spirit message, consisting of garbled fragments of biblical teaching, only leaves the hearer mystified. Notably absent from the discourse—despite Betty's own Christian confession—is any solid biblical content or the clear confession of Jesus Christ as Lord. On yet another occasion Betty's asking an entity named Joohop, "Why doesn't man love others all the time?" is an opportune time for the aliens to confess the biblical truth about man's sinful nature. Instead, we are treated to an obtuse discourse straight out of Eastern mysticism:

"Because man has separated himself," he said, "he has become dual. Separation, duality. He has formed that other side. He has made it to happen. It was all good at one time.

Even his choice was good at one time. He has separated it.
In love there is no separation."[9]

Salvation, according to Eastern thought, has nothing
to do with biblical teaching about sin and redemption.
Rather, man is inherently divine and has somehow become
separated from *Brahma,* the impersonal force from which
the universe has arisen. The temporary dualism between
matter and spirit will be resolved after interminable re-
incarnations, when man's spiritual nature finally succeeds
in merging with the divine. In Taoist thought the illusion
of dualism is expressed by *yin-yang,* light and darkness.
Even the dark side, according to Taoism, has its purpose,
which is eventually to synthesize with the side of light.

In this regard, the statements by Andreasson's aliens
about separation and duality betray their opposition to
the worldview of Christianity. And they help us understand the observation of Whitley Strieber (who looks to
Taoism to explain his own abduction experiences) that
Andreasson's faith "is far more pure than the twisted remnant that passes for modern fundamentalism."[10]

Masters of Deception

Returning to the related phenomenon of angelic visitations, we have seen that, although some recorded incidents might be genuine, others are outright demonic.
Despite a convincing appearance as heavenly angels (such
as in the experience of Betty Eadie), a closer examination
of what they say or teach reveals that they are not from
God.

We know that Satan and his demons are capable of dis-
guising themselves as angels of light, as well as appearing in more unpleasant forms. They have the ability to
manipulate the minds and senses of men and women so
as to convince them that they are seeing and experienc-

ing utterly fantastic creatures and their "spacecrafts" in other-dimensional places. We have seen that Satan's minions may even be able to form temporal manifestations in the atmosphere and in close proximity to their victims. The purpose of these apparitions is to support the overarching deception that humankind is being visited by intelligent beings from elsewhere in the universe.

We have every reason, moreover, to expect the *expansion* of the parameters of this deception being perpetrated on the human race. It may well be that one day we will see overt manifestations of UFO activity of a far greater magnitude than we have observed thus far. Does that sound far-fetched? It will mean nothing less than an earth-shaking challenge to the comfortable worldview of many. The "theological aspects" of the UFO phenomena, as J. Allen Hynek predicted, will "constitute a challenge to our present belief systems."[11]

But Hynek is equivocating here. Exactly which belief systems will be challenged? Not those of occultism or Eastern religions. Those, as John Mack notes approvingly, "have always recognized a vast range of spirit entities in the cosmos."[12] The adherents of an Eastern-occult worldview, which has no place for the God of Judeo-Christian monotheism, have no difficulty accepting a universe filled with spirit beings, because for them the universe itself is divine.

No, the belief system that will be challenged is, pure and simple, that of Christianity.

Conclusion

There is an ominous ramification for all this: Religious or philosophical worldviews that have no room for the God of the Bible also tend to have little tolerance for those who do. There will come a time, perhaps not too far from now, when the Antichrist will embark on a ruthless campaign to rid the earth of those who believe in the one true God and in His Son, Jesus. To accomplish this he will have at his disposal spiritual powers that invoke powerful displays of supernatural phenomena.

We have seen how UFOs and aliens may well play a part in this end-time drama. Regardless of whether you or I will be present for that final, end-time deception, none of us is immune from attack in the here and now by spiritual forces in heavenly places.

And so we return to the question we raised at the beginning of this chapter: Why are some, like Marge, spared tragedy, while others, like Betty Andreasson, are not? Ultimately, of course, there is no answer to this question apart from the sovereignty of God. But part of the answer lies in personal knowledge of God's eternal Son, Jesus Christ, and in spiritual preparedness.

The question for each of us to answer is, Are we prepared spiritually? Are we experiencing victory over the assaults of the enemy *now?* Betty Andreasson, unlike Marge, was not. We can sympathize with her vain pleading for protection over a period of many years (as bizarre as her story is) as aliens forced their way into her life.

Assuming that she offers her accounts in honesty and sincerity, why were such creatures allowed to subject her to such experiences? And how can each of us avoid the same pitfalls and rest in the confidence of divine protection from evil attack?

14

Keep Looking Up!

e learn from Jesus Himself how to avoid the pitfalls we have seen in the unfortunate case of Betty Andreasson:

> Not everyone who says to me, "Lord, Lord," will enter the kingdom of heaven, but only he who does the will of my Father who is in heaven. Many will say to me on that day, "Lord, Lord, did we not prophesy in your name, and in your name drive out demons and perform many miracles?" Then I will tell them plainly, "I never knew you. Away from me, you evildoers!"
>
> Matthew 7:21–23

These are difficult words to accept. Can Jesus be against people who are well-meaning? The answer, of course, is that Jesus seeks to nurture even the weakest faith, as foretold by the prophet: "A bruised reed he will not break, and a smoldering wick he will not snuff out" (Matthew 12:20). But Jesus is warning those who lack any genuine faith.

The fact that they were performing miracles on their own, not commissioned by Jesus, cannot in itself be the reason they were rejected. In another place Jesus' disciples inform Him of just such a person:

> "Master," said John, "we saw a man driving out demons in your name and we tried to stop him, because he is not one of us." "Do not stop him," Jesus said, "for whoever is not against you is for you."
>
> Luke 9:49–50

Jesus expressed surprising tolerance for those beyond the circle of His disciples who had the audacity to perform miracles in His name. We should exhibit the same attitude toward those outside our own circle and our own way of doing things who are nonetheless serving the same Lord. It is not a question of maverick followers; the explanation lies in Jesus' last phrase: "*I never knew you.* Away from me, you evildoers!"

As happy as I am to see people on their way to church on Sunday, many parishioners proud of lifelong membership in a particular church will fall under the condemnation of Jesus. On the Day of Judgment there will be no recitations from church membership rolls or flourishing of baptismal certificates as admission tickets to heaven. There will be no boasting about faithful attendance, positions held or services performed. Altar boy, vicar and homeless alcoholic sneaking in to warm himself in the vestibule will all stand together shoulder to shoulder in one speechless, awestruck company.

Only one book of records will be brought forth, to which every spellbound eye will turn, for it holds the key to eternal life or death: "If anyone's name was not found written in the book of life, he was thrown into the lake of fire" (Revelation 20:15).

The heart of Christianity is personal faith in Jesus Christ as Lord and Savior. Those in a saving relationship with Jesus have their names written in the Book of Life. Jesus tells His disciples to "rejoice that your names are written in heaven" (Luke 10:20). Likewise, the apostle Paul speaks of his fellow workers "whose names are in the book of life" (Philippians 4:3).

Not one of us, of course, can judge Betty Andreasson's spiritual condition. But Jesus warned in the passage we just looked at that "many" on the Day of Judgment will be found wanting. Tragically they will lose out on eternal life because they lack a personal relationship with the Lord Jesus and are not known by Him.

Is it that we have a harsh, unloving God who delights in judgment? Far from it! Rather, "He is patient with you, not wanting anyone to perish, but everyone to come to repentance" (2 Peter 3:9). The basis of condemnation, therefore, will be a person's own refusal to repent and accept the free gift of salvation in Jesus Christ.

Our Divine Protection Plan

Trusting Jesus Christ as our personal Savior conveys a wondrous blessing: "To all who received him, to those who believed in his name, he gave the right to become children of God" (John 1:12). Just as youngsters assume their fathers will protect them, we have the right as God's children to call on Him for spiritual protection.

Obviously Christians are not immune from sickness, crime, disasters or a myriad other evils. But we can prayerfully trust that we will be spared (perhaps unknowingly) much evil: "A thousand may fall at your side, ten thousand at your right hand, but it will not come near you" (Psalm 91:7). The ninety-first psalm contains another wonderful promise of divine safekeeping: "For he will

command his angels concerning you to guard you in all
your ways" (verse 11).

Those Who Trust in God

Can we always expect such angelic protection? Betty
Eadie and many of her readers assume that everyone—
even the religious skeptic and atheist—is equally eligible
for divine refuge.

The psalmist, however, is speaking of those who put
their trust in the living God, who say, "He is my refuge
and my fortress, my God, in whom I trust" (verse 2). The
Lord (as we read later in the same psalm) reciprocates
that devotion and trust: "'Because he loves me,' says the
LORD, 'I will rescue him; I will protect him, for he
acknowledges my name'" (91:14). Thus, while in God's
mercy even nonbelievers are often spared calamity, it is
people who acknowledge and submit to Him who can
expect divine protection.

We may perhaps dare to ask, What would have happened to Marge if she were not walking with the Lord
and attuned to His voice that day? But at the same time
we must be careful not to assume that dedicated Christians will escape all evil and tragedy. Experience tells
us otherwise. We live in a fallen world and are subject
to the effects of sin.

It is only one future day, in the "new heaven and new
earth" promised in Revelation 21:1, that we will at long
last be freed from the effects of sin, when "the creation
itself will be liberated from its bondage to decay and
brought into the glorious freedom of the children of God"
(Romans 8:21).

What about spiritual attacks of the sort experienced
by those who claim to be alien abductees? This is quite
another matter. There is no warrant whatsoever for Christians to have to suffer demonic oppression:

In righteousness you will be established: Tyranny will be far
from you; you will have nothing to fear. Terror will be far
removed; it will not come near you.

Isaiah 54:14

Those Who Rebel against God

There is no corresponding promise in Scripture offered
to those who are living in rebellion against God. They can
expect no defense in time of trouble: "What will you do
on the day of reckoning, when disaster comes from afar?
To whom will you run for help?" (Isaiah 10:3).

Whitley Strieber had no basis on which to plead for
divine protection, even if he were prepared to ask for it.
In one terrifying abduction sequence, when the aliens were
about to insert a strange instrument into his brain, he
protested loudly, "I'm not gonna let you do an operation
on me. You have absolutely no right."

The blunt reply came back: "We do have a right."[1]

The New Testament has much to say about spiritual
darkness. Unbelievers, unlike God's children, who have
been "rescued . . . from the dominion of darkness" (Colos-
sians 1:13), have no spiritual protection or shield against
the enemy.

Los Angeles Christian journalist Stuart Goldman, in
discussing the backgrounds of UFO abductees, notes that
"it quickly becomes clear that almost to a man, they have
some background in New Age or occultic beliefs. Interestingly, studies show that there are very few practicing
Christians or Jews among UFO contactees."[2]

It is not necessary to be involved directly in the occult
to be fair game for demonic forces. Barney and Betty Hill
were Unitarians, a religious denomination that rejects the
foundational teachings of Christianity such as the Trinity and the deity, substitutionary atonement, resurrection
and the Second Coming of Jesus Christ.

Accounts of demonic abduction like those we have examined confirm the apostle's warning: "Mark this: There will be terrible times in the last days" (2 Timothy 3:1). The world is in the throes of a ferocious spiritual battle that will only intensify as we approach the climax of human history. Whether or not we are attuned to the idea, Christians are vital participants in this cosmic struggle and are commanded to be prepared:

> Finally, be strong in the Lord and in his mighty power. Put on the full armor of God so that you can take your stand against the devil's schemes. For our struggle is not against flesh and blood, but against the rulers, against the authorities, against the powers of this dark world and against the spiritual forces of evil in the heavenly realms. Therefore put on the full armor of God, so that when the day of evil comes, you may be able to stand your ground, and after you have done everything, to stand.
>
> Ephesians 6:10–13

To attempt to go into spiritual battle equipped with anything less than "the full armor of God" would be no more effectual than attacking an armored tank with a slingshot. Will we be prepared when our hour of testing comes?

Those who find that they lack divine protection when under spiritual attack should, in the words of the apostle Paul, "examine yourselves to see whether you are in the faith; test yourselves. Do you not realize that Christ Jesus is in you—unless, of course, you fail the test?" (2 Corinthians 13:5).

God's Children Who Are Disobedient

It is not only unbelievers, unfortunately, who come under fierce spiritual attack and find themselves living in continual defeat. Christians, too, who profess to love the

Lord are often enslaved by "besetting sins" that the evil
one uses to keep their effectiveness to a minimum. God
desires—and expects—that our lives not be stained with
unrepentant sin:

> It is God's will that you should be holy; that you should
> avoid sexual immorality; that each of you should learn to
> control his own body in a way that is holy and honorable.
>
> 1 Thessalonians 4:3–4

If we continue in practices we know to be sinful, we
can expect the correction of our heavenly Father:

> "My son, do not make light of the Lord's discipline, and do
> not lose heart when he rebukes you, because the Lord dis-
> ciplines those he loves, and he punishes everyone he accepts
> as a son."
>
> Hebrews 12:5–6

The Lord's discipline is meant not for our condemnation but for our good, for true happiness is found only in
complete submission to Him. Nor is there any other way
we can hope to be overcomers in the evil days to come.
The following practical steps can help anyone who feels
in some way that he or she has been taken captive by the
evil one:[3]

1. *Renew your first love.* To be ready to meet Christ
   when He comes, you cannot be lukewarm or serving Him halfheartedly. Do not let your heart be
   divided between Christ and the world.

2. *Repent.* Confess and turn away from any coldness,
   lukewarmness or indifference to spiritual matters.
   Ask God to reveal any sin or disobedience in your
   life. Then confess it and determine that with God's
   help you will be defeated no longer.

3. *Cleanse yourself.* We must put to death our fleshly desires. Take authority over ungodly or lustful thoughts and keep your conversation wholesome. Speak only what will build up people around you.

4. *Adorn yourself.* No one will sit down at the Marriage Supper of the Lamb without being clothed with the wedding garment of righteousness. Christ's righteousness is ours by faith, but we must live a holy, separated life through the power of the Holy Spirit.

5. *Be on guard.* We need to be ready spiritually to face the onslaught of the enemy. Satan is unleashing his fury on God's people because he knows his time is limited. We must be on guard, ready to face and defeat him.

6. *Do the will of God.* Be faithful in the work God has called you to do. Put His work first and focus your heart and mind on accomplishing it instead of fulfilling your own desires.

7. *Don't give up.* Many have become weary from the difficulties and battles they face. We must persevere during trials and adversity. Do not lose hope; our steadfastness will not be in vain.

By Invitation Only

If you realize that in some area you are lacking, the remedy is not far away. Jesus is waiting for us to respond to Him:

> "Here I am! I stand at the door and knock. If anyone hears my voice and opens the door, I will come in and eat with him, and he with me."

> Revelation 3:20

This verse is pregnant with meaning for those living in the Middle East, where hospitality is held in high regard. This offer of Jesus, viewed in its cultural setting, is one of intimate friendship. He stands outside, waiting patiently.

What a contrast with the cursed emissaries of hell, pushing into people's lives and subjecting them to horrific experiences, while all along assuring them and their "alien apologists" that they are interested in our well-being!

Jesus waits for us to surrender our hearts to Him. If we steadfastly refuse, to whom will we turn for help and protection during the dark night of our souls? There will be no one else to blame when our desperate cries of "Lord! Lord!" go unheeded. No, let us heed the admonition of the apostle Paul: "I tell you, now is the time of God's favor, now is the day of salvation" (2 Corinthians 6:2).

The End of the Story

People everywhere are searching for miraculous help for the problems they face. The popular angel literature crammed into most bookstores is replete with examples of those who have called on the name of the Lord in time of dire need—sometimes with miraculous results. Even when we weed out the questionable accounts, we still have ample reason to be encouraged that divine protection is just a prayer away.

Take the well-known case of John Patton and his wife, pioneer missionaries to the New Hebrides Islands. The young couple found themselves the objects of increasing opposition, to the point that they feared for their lives. Still they persevered in their efforts to reach the people of the island with the Gospel.

One night things came to a head, and they heard a great commotion outside their small missionary compound. As retold in Marilynn Carlson Webber's book *A Rustle of*

Angels, the Pattons discovered that their worst fears had come true:

> Looking out, they saw they were completely surrounded by the chief and his men with torches and spears. They were being true to their word. They had come to burn their home and kill the missionaries. The Pattons had no weapons. There was no earthly means of protection, but they could pray, and pray they did! Throughout the terror-filled night they prayed that this warlike tribe would someday find peace with God.[4]

As dawn broke the tribe drifted away. The Pattons were both greatly relieved and puzzled at the departure of the angry tribesmen. But despite the troubling incident, they persisted in their work with no further incidents.

A full year passed. Then one day their steadfast efforts paid off and the chief of the tribe became a Christian. Now was their chance to learn the rest of the story. They asked the chief why he and his men had come to the missionary compound that fateful night the previous year. Webber recounts his answer:

> "We came to kill you and burn everything you have."
>
> "What kept you from doing it?" the missionary asked.
>
> "We were afraid of all those men who were guarding your house," the chief replied.
>
> "But there were no men," Patton replied. "We were alone, my wife and I."
>
> "No, no," the chief insisted. "There were many men around your house. Big men. Giants. They were awesome. They had no torches but they glowed with a strange light, and each had a drawn sword in his hand. Who were they?"[5]

Make no mistake about it: The mighty warriors guarding the Pattons' house that night were the real thing— angels sent from God to protect His people. They were worlds apart from despicable beings hiding in the shadows who come to wreak havoc and terrorize their victims. One thing is certain: When it comes to the last battle, it will be no contest.

The Pattons rejoiced to learn the rest of their story; and we have come to the end of ours.

What will be the end, my friend, of *your* story?

Appendix: A Review of Texe Marrs' *Dark Majesty*

Some readers with a special interest in conspiracy theories would like this issue addressed in more detail. Accordingly, I am dedicating this appendix especially to "conspiracy buffs" who (perhaps alone!) can tolerate such detailed information.

The best way to highlight some concerns about the subject may be to take a look at a recent book by Texe Marrs, whose titles have reportedly sold more than one million to date. Marrs, a former U.S. Air Force officer and professor of aerospace studies, has written several books exposing the growing influence of New Age philosophy. Marrs' book *Dark Majesty* reflects his disturbing thesis:

> Is there behind the scenes an Illuminati, a secret clique of wealthy men masterminding a massive conspiracy to rule the world? Are these powerful and influential men behind the frenzied campaign for World Government and a New International Economic Order?[1]

page ix

Marrs does not leave the reader guessing for long. A few pages later he states his unambiguous conclusion:

> Once you read this book, you will know for a certainty—if you don't already know it—that there is a World Conspiracy by a hidden elite. You will just know it. Period. All the evidence is there—mountains of evidence. No other conclusion is possible. A World Conspiracy that deeply and severely affects you and me exists. It is for real.
>
> page xii

That does not leave much room for maneuvering.

I will be equally forthright and state my opinion of this book at the outset: It has strengths and serious weaknesses. Let's begin with a genuinely positive aspect of the book that should not be overlooked: Marrs does a good job describing the essence of occultism and its pervasive anti-Christian mindset.

A Clear and Present Danger

Many Christians have little or no idea that the massive and growing amalgam of New Age organizations has one primary objective: the suppression of Christianity. Forget about ecology, saving the whales, holistic thinking, eliminating world hunger, raising consciousness levels and a myriad other purported causes. The same underlying philosophy drives all these groups: a worldview unremittingly hostile to Christianity.

This does not mean that every group mentioned in *Dark Majesty* is prepared to burn Christians at the stake. Far be it from many of them who (thanks to the residual but powerful restraining influence of Christian culture) prefer consciousness-raising to coercion. Yet the ominous thread is there, and it follows all too logically from occultism and Eastern mysticism.

Toward the end of *Dark Majesty* Marrs hits this point effectively, and I take my hat off to him. It is a point worth focusing on. In a section entitled "Beware of Inferior Subhuman Species," he gives the reader a shocking but accurate description of the general New Age attitude toward Christianity:

> Regrettably, the mind controllers carefully explain, there are some people in this world who are of an inferior species. These subhumans are a cancerous stain on humanity. They are the ones responsible for all the world's ills. The subhuman species, the claim goes, is polluting our rivers and oceans, and cutting down millennia-old forests with reckless abandon. The unfit ones are teaching the children of earth that they must stay bound to the old traditionalist religions such as Biblical Christianity. . . .
>
> pages 230–231

How to solve this problem is a ticklish question for those still steeped in the Judeo-Christian respect for individual rights that permeates Western society. One New Age theorist addresses this issue delicately:

> From the point of view of governments, rule by fear and torture must be a messy affair, generating problems of its own. It would be much simpler if techniques existed to make people want to behave in the desired way.[2]

The Soviet dissident poet V. I. Chernyshov knew all too well about such techniques whereby uncooperative members of society were imprisoned in mental hospitals and injected with powerful and dangerous drugs for the purpose of "curing" their "mental illness." Chernyshov noted that many of his fellow prisoners were Christians guilty of no crime other than desiring to practice their faith. His final communication to the outside world revealed his most desperate fear:

I'm terribly afraid of torture. But there is a worse torture . . .
the introduction of chemicals into my mind. . . . I have
already been informed of the decision for my treatment.
Farewell.[3]

But hold on! Isn't it reckless to make a glib connection
between the run-of-the-mill New Age group and the monstrous tactics of the Soviet secret police, or stretching things
to imply that such things are even being contemplated?
I wish it were. Listen to this mind-boggling statement
by Professor Chester Pierce of Harvard University's
Department of Educational Psychiatry in a speech to a
national teachers convention:

> Every child of America entering school at the age of five is
> mentally ill, because he comes to school with certain alle-
> giances toward his founding fathers, toward his elected offi-
> cials, toward his parents, toward a belief in a supernatural
> being, toward the sovereignty of the nation as a separate
> entity. It's up to you teachers to make all these children well,
> by creating international children of the future.[4]

This was no crackpot spouting threats to no one in particular. A professor from one of the most respected institutions of higher learning in the world was exhorting this
nation's teachers to cure the "mental illness" of their students. Notice what Dr. Pierce considered the cause of this
mental illness: belief in God and allegiance toward parents, government and country.

We may choose to turn off this information, refusing
to believe it could be true. There must be some explanation. The speaker is not representative. He is not really
advocating what amounts to persecution for Christian
beliefs. The author must have distorted the evidence to
prove his alarmist point. And so on.

But for others the troubling realization begins to dawn concerning a prediction of Jesus regarding His followers:

> "Blessed are you when men hate you, when they exclude you and insult you and reject your name as evil, because of the Son of Man."
>
> Luke 6:22

The apostle Paul echoes this:

> In fact, everyone who wants to live a godly life in Christ Jesus will be persecuted.
>
> 2 Timothy 3:12

Most of us do not personalize these predictions. They are words we secretly hope will never come to pass for us in our lifetimes.

But we do ourselves a disservice to refuse to face up to age-old concerted enmity toward the Church of Jesus Christ. It is an issue Texe Marrs addresses forthrightly in *Dark Majesty* and which, if left at that, would make the book valuable reading for Christians.

The Secret Brotherhood

Regrettably, the book does not stop with these observations, but descends into a morass of conspiracy beliefs that has doubtless left many readers agitated and confused by frightening—yet all too often unsubstantiated—assertions.

Dark Majesty begins innocently enough, as Texe Marrs describes his own earlier reluctance to believe in the existence of a secret group of men he calls the "Secret Brotherhood":

> Frankly, during the first 42 years or so of my life, I did not believe that such a group of men existed. I found the con- spiracy "theory" of history somewhat amusing, if not

absurd. When I encountered otherwise highly intelligent people who seemed to be consumed by notions of a hidden conspiracy of international bankers bent on ruling the world, I
typically put them in the category of either bizarre eccentrics
or, quite possibly, nuts and overly bright wackos. "Surely,"
I thought, "their research and findings must be marred and
their conclusions defective."

pages ix–x

Statements like these have the effect of disarming the
reader, who will likely identify. But the author moves
quickly beyond such skepticism, and it is hard to miss the
message that only those who want to stick their heads in
the sand can deny Marrs' conclusions. What follows is
page after page, chapter after chapter, of astounding claims
about an immense worldwide conspiracy:

I'm convinced from my research and the evidence that God
has allowed to come my way over the last six years that . . .
these groups are linked together. They are networking. Moreover, there is, in fact, an elite, a clique, at the very top. You
can call it an invisible college, you can call it an invisible
order, some have called it the "hidden hand"; but there is a
powerful and centrally located leadership unit.

page 148

The Skull & Bones Society

Part of the information Marrs presents that is undeni-
ably true includes several chapters devoted to a secretive
society at Yale University formally registered as The Russell Trust. He accords this organization, otherwise known
as "Skull & Bones," a special preeminence in the shadowy conspiratorial network:

Now, of all the influential secret societies and orders that I
have come across, the Skull & Bones Society seems to enjoy

unusual prominence and authority. The Skull & Bones has infiltrated and penetrated almost every area of our society.

page 148

The existence of this society and its peculiar hazing rites have been exposed elsewhere, as has the fact that the elite membership of Skull & Bones (only fifteen upperclassmen at Yale chosen each year) are often assisted on their way to career and financial success by well-placed alumni "Bonesmen" in the upper echelons of the business world.

Marrs dwells at length on former President George Bush's membership in Skull & Bones while an undergrad at Yale in the late 1940s. It does seem plausible, as the book alleges, that the former president's career in the oil industry and later in politics received boosts at critical junctures by other alumni Bonesmen. According to Marrs, however, Skull & Bones does not act in a vacuum but with concerted purpose.

He goes on to probe the relationship between Skull & Bones and the inner circle of occultists of the Illuminati (or, as Marrs calls it, the Secret Brotherhood):

> We have seen the immense influence of the Skull & Bones in every area of American society. But is this secretive and integral part of a network of organizations and secret societies founded and controlled from above by a concealed and even more secretive higher authority?

page 206

It is clear that Marrs answers this question in the affirmative. To demonstrate, he presents a long list of prestigious Bonesmen in government and other high places of influence stretching back to the founding of the Russell Trust in 1832.

Here is where cracks begin to show in Marrs' speculations. He devotes much space to lists and descriptions of these persons and how each in turn did his part to weaken the fabric of American society. He also assumes, though he never establishes the connection, that all these Bonesmen were in the service of the Secret Brotherhood. The documentation appears impressive. (The author would call it indisputable.) The problem is that the average reader is not in a position to investigate these claims, but can only trust that Marrs has done his homework and is presenting the facts accurately.

The Revolving Doors at 1600 Pennsylvania Avenue

Dark Majesty attempts to show how the alleged conspiracy pulls the strings behind the scenes of American politics, right up to and including the office of President of the United States. But by the time the reader works through the confusing and contradictory account of how this manipulation and control allegedly transpires, he will probably be more bewildered than when he began.

Take Richard Nixon. It was Nixon, according to Marrs, "who, as president, played a key role in catapulting the young Bonesman [George Bush] to the top of the political heap. In turn, Richard Nixon's chief mentor and backer was David Rockefeller." Later Marrs calls Nixon "a puppet of the Rockefeller-Kissinger monied interests, who became George Bush's undercover 'Godfather' in the 1970's." Billionaire Rockefeller, according to Marrs, is one of the world's "chief power brokers" who has "through his minions and insiders in the Oval Office of the White House, successfully manipulated the foreign and economic policies of the United States for a quarter of a century—or more" (pp. 28, 30, 173).

Dark Majesty implies that this elite group of financiers either constitutes the Illuminati/Secret Brotherhood or is closely aligned with it and exercises an astounding degree of control over mankind. In referring to a book by French politician Jacques Attali (but not documenting it), Marrs poses a rhetorical question:

> Can this much power really be wielded over the common man by the international financiers? Attali provides astonishing information, consistent with all the research I have done on the conspiracy, that the men at the top actually have such vast, encompassing power and influence that they become superintendents of all other men on this planet.
>
> page 64

Superintendents of all other men on this planet? If you are waiting to learn more, you will be disappointed. Except for one brief quotation, Marrs does not enlighten his readers any further concerning Attali's book. Is this because what Attali has to say would be too mind-boggling for the average reader, or because there is no substantiation?

But back to Nixon—and here is where the confusion is compounded. If Rockefeller and the international financiers hold such "vast, encompassing power and influence," why could they not prevent Nixon's ignoble fall from the presidency as a result of the Watergate coverup? Surely it would have been within their power to suppress the Congressional investigation—unless they had changed their minds about Nixon, or unless they are not as omnipotent as *Dark Majesty* makes them out to be.

Things get more perplexing when Marrs discusses the 1980 presidential election between incumbent Jimmy Carter and contender Ronald Reagan. The real power-broker in the Reagan camp, according to Marrs, was political strategist William Casey, later head of the CIA:

> In reality, Casey was a Brotherhood mole, a special undercover agent inside the Reagan campaign organization. It was William Casey who would see to it that the Reagan administration was packed with appointees from the internation-

alist Council on Foreign Relations and the Trilateral Commission. But first . . . [he needed] . . . to make sure that his man, Ronald Reagan, then leading in the polls, would not be defeated in November by incumbent Jimmy Carter. . . .

pages 178–179

So far, so good. We know by now that the Council on Foreign Relations and the Trilateral Commission are supposed to be front organizations for the Secret Brotherhood. It makes sense that they would steamroll over anyone, including the President of the United States, who stood in their way. But Marrs states earlier that "both Jimmy Carter and Henry Kissinger have long been active members of this same group." What group? None other than The Trilateral Commission (p. 28)!

Why would the all-powerful conspiracy dispose of one of their own whom they had already placed in the most powerful office on earth? Marrs does not elaborate, but Jimmy Carter's "miraculous" association with the CFR and TLC and subsequent rise to power was a recurring theme in the conspiracy literature of the mid–1970s.

We are confronted with two possibilities to explain this. First, that both Carter and Kissinger blew it and were engineered out of office by the Secret Brotherhood. But where is the evidence for that? What offenses did they commit? Marrs does not address this, nor does he acknowledge the contradiction. Indeed, the conspiracy theory blithely skips over this anomaly.

The other possibility is that, once again, the Illuminati/Secret Brotherhood is not as omnipotent as the conspiracy theorists would have us believe. Even though it contradicts his own speculations, Marrs admits this himself in so many words in explaining Ronald Reagan's victory in the 1980 Republican primary:

To the chagrin of the financial wizards who comprise the Brotherhood, George [Bush] was soundly defeated by the former Hollywood actor from California in the primary campaigns. Reagan, the Great Communicator, was not to be denied. The common people rallied to his side. . . .

page 177

But we were just told that the Secret Brotherhood was managing Ronald Reagan's campaign through their "mole" William Casey. So why were they chagrined when Reagan won?[5]

Besides that contradiction, it is perplexing that the grandiose schemes of the Brotherhood were somehow thwarted by the common people who voted Reagan in, especially when we have been assured that the men at the top have such vast, encompassing power and influence that they directly or indirectly control everyone on planet earth.

Time fails us to discuss every politician mentioned in *Dark Majesty* said to be controlled by the Secret Brotherhood. Marrs gives much attention to the career of former President George Bush, called the "ultimate insider," who works directly for "his bosses in the Brotherhood" (p. 30).

When I read this I flipped to the front of the book. Sure enough, *Dark Majesty* was released in 1992, *before* the November elections. If Marrs had known President Bush would go down in defeat at the polls, would he have spent so much time in the book presenting Bush as the Secret Brotherhood's ultimate waterboy? President Bill Clinton, by contrast, merits only a passing mention.

In what may be one of his most dubious assertions, Marrs picks Dan Quayle as the next rising star of the conspiratorialists:

Vice President Dan Quayle is another fair-haired boy of the wealthy Bilderberger supermen. Quayle was there in person last year at the gathering. Reportedly David Rockefeller and

fellow big-wigs were duly impressed at what they saw. "He's our man—for '96 or sooner!" one Bilderberger exclaimed.
                              page 102 (quoting unspecified sources)

This revelation must come as quite a shock to those familiar with Dan Quayle's unabashedly pro-family and conservative morality positions and who witnessed the relentless media-bashing Quayle endured throughout his tenure (though not since). But it highlights one effect of becoming immersed in conspiracy theories: It is easy to become convinced that no one can be trusted to be who he says he is. Virtually everyone who holds political power, from the President of the United States down to the local city council member, is potentially a secret "mole" of the Illuminati.

Pro- or Anti-Communist?

Standard conspiracy theory has it that the international financiers and others behind the world conspiracy supported Vladimir Lenin and helped to create the Marxist, atheistic Soviet Union. The reasons they did so are convoluted and unclear, but it is claimed, in some unfathomable way, that the creation of an enormously powerful Marxist, atheistic state was part of "the Plan." In *Dark Majesty* Marrs passes along this idea uncritically:

> We also should not forget the emergence of a communist dictatorship, Lenin's vanguard, in Moscow in 1917. Lenin, and subsequently Joseph Stalin, were co-partners in a conspiratorial scheme that at first consisted of only a handful of determined and ruthless Marxists. They were funded behind the scenes by secret societies and others in Germany and America. Their repugnant campaign to purify Mother Russia and to seek world domination resulted in possibly as many as 100 million human beings wiped out and brutally purged and eliminated in a brief space of 76 years.
>   page 47

Let me interject that considerable evidence exists to support the allegation that Western financiers did help prop up the Soviet Union from the very beginning. It is no secret that large loans were made to Russia through the decades facilitated by the international banking community.

It is a primary strategy of international bankers and industrialists to strengthen the economies of underdeveloped countries and raise their standard of living. This is accomplished primarily through multinational financial organizations such as the World Bank and the International Monetary Fund. Why? Because countries with a low standard of living cannot afford to purchase Western goods.

International bankers wanted to bring the Soviet Union (despite a hopeless political system) into financial dependence on the West, requiring and desiring ever more Western goods and services, at which point the natural resources and economic potential of that vast land could be exploited. Call it capitalist greed. It was certainly in many ways a misguided and wasteful approach; at the time of its collapse the Soviet Union was many tens of billions of dollars in debt to the West.

But the same scenario is played out today in dozens of underdeveloped countries, and it is not necessary to postulate that it is being orchestrated by a highly secret Illuminati.

Marrs, undeterred, takes this as undeniable proof of the hidden hand of the Secret Brotherhood: "How amazing, then, that some today deny that a conspiracy could possibly exist!" (p. 47).

Back to pro- or anti-Communism. Once again things become confused and contradictory:

All of these planks of the Brotherhood's plan have enjoyed shockingly accurate fulfillment: the surprising, recent developments in the formation of the Europe Economic Community, President George Bush's proposal of a North American Free Trade Zone, and the resounding fall of communism and breakup of the Soviet Union. . . .

page 44

But weren't we told that the Secret Brotherhood conspiracy virtually created and sustained the Soviet Union? Now we are told that members of the conspiracy were elated at the dismantling of that selfsame Soviet empire:

> What a revolution we have experienced! The seeming dissolution and freeing up of Communist Eastern Europe, as well as Gorbachev's Perestroika and Glasnost policies inside the Soviet Union, have resulted in a euphoric mania of One Worldism. Finally, exclaim gleeful globalists, finally [sic] we can have a unified and harmonious One World Order.

page 111

A few years ago such backflips would have been unnecessary. Few predicted the sudden collapse of Communism. But times have changed, and the conspiracy theories must change with the times. Thus, we are now told with hindsight that the Secret Brotherhood was actually working for the *downfall* of the Soviet Union.

The Theory with a Thousand Faces

Let me be honest: I am open in principle to the existence of shadowy conspiratorial organizations like the Illuminati. But in terms of solid evidence, books like *Dark Majesty* fail to deliver. For all the hype, pinning down specific proof about the alleged Secret Brotherhood is like trying to nail Jell-O to the wall.

Unfortunately, the lack of documentation plays right into the hands of those who assure us that an organized conspiracy exists. The reader is obliged to swallow outright contradictions and constantly shifting "proofs." This only demonstrates (we are told) how deep and profound the conspiracy actually is.

The inconsistencies we have just discussed regarding the relationship between the Illuminati and the worldwide Communist movement are a prime example of the adaptability of conspiracy theories. The inner circle of the Secret Brotherhood is, we are repeatedly told, far too secretive for the average citizen to fathom. Since Marrs reveals no documented facts about the top leadership, including their identities, there is no way we can critique what we are told.

Curiously, even those purportedly exposing the conspiracy seem to relish their role as dispensers of privileged information. In one tantalizing passage Marrs gives his readers the impression he has inside information about the inner circle:

> All of these groups—and many more which we will expose—are part of one gigantic, unified, global network known collectively as the Secret Brotherhood. In the past they have also been identified as the Illuminati. And at the top, at the very pinnacle of this network, is a hidden combine: a small clique, or committee, of plotters. Currently there are nine illuminized men who sit on this exclusive committee. Eventually a tenth will join them, but for now his seat becomes vacant.
>
> page 18

It sounds as though Marrs has inside information about who these nine men are. Indeed, he continues to throw out fascinating tidbits about this group of nine men at the very center of the worldwide conspiracy:

> These nine men possess more power and authority than any other group in all of human history. They meet regularly at

various locations around the globe and plot out the future of the world and humanity. Once they make a decision or set a policy, the entire apparatus of the Secret Brotherhood snaps together to implement it, like some piece of complex, intricate, well-oiled machinery.

pages 18–19

So who are they? Marrs gives the impression of knowing firsthand how they operate. But nowhere in *Dark Majesty*, which purports to "unravel the whole fantastic story of the men who have been called the Illuminati," does Marrs oblige his readers with any documentation or any inkling as to their identities. The inner circle remains obscure, and the reader's frustration increases with every page, although exposing the worldwide conspiracy is the stated concern of the book:

Those of us who truly care about truth and about freedom, liberty, and the future of our country can do something to stem the tidal wave of occultism and propaganda sponsored by these men and their associates. If it be God's will, *we can* restore the world to sanity and goodness. But the first thing to be done is to unmask the plot of the Secret Brotherhood and shed some much needed light on their dangerous, often disguised activities.

page 34 (original italics)

Why does *Dark Majesty* not unmask the nine men and reveal their identities? Is it because Marrs chooses not to divulge their names, or because his research amounts to hearsay and unsubstantiated allegations and he has nothing more concrete to offer?

Perhaps in order to justify the dearth of facts, apart from the standard, oft-repeated rhetoric of conspiracy writers, Marrs gives a novel reason as to why we are left in the dark:

To confuse and cover-up their criminal and conspiratorial activity, the arrogant elite trained in the use of alchemy and magic purposely create disinformation traps and mental obstacles and fruitless paths which, they believe, the uninitiated cannot navigate.

page 127

And again:

The story of how an international cartel of super-rich conspirators have been able to induce a form of delusion and hallucination into the minds of men is almost too fantastic to believe.

page 227

It *is* almost too fantastic to believe, especially later when we read about inducing "a form of group insanity and planetary delusion" (p. 261). If such stunning—and unsubstantiated—assertions are to be believed, then the vast majority of humankind is muffled in an impenetrable fog of disinformation and mental obstacles.

How is it possible that the Illuminati are able to blanket the world in ignorance concerning their true aims? Marrs offers an even more astounding explanation:

The elitists who comprise the Secret Brotherhood are without exception initiates of secret societies. . . . The concealed men of the magnificently powerful Secret Brotherhood are, in fact, blood brothers whose minds have long been immersed and shrouded in a magical paradigm totally incomprehensible to the common man.

page 71

Once again Marrs intimates that he knows who these men are—but why does he not name them? And here the cracks in the standard conspiracy theories become fissures. We have been told repeatedly that the inner circle of the conspiracy possesses vast, unstoppable power that none can defeat. We have been told that the members employ prodigious magical powers, keeping humankind effectively in the dark and preventing their Plan from being thwarted.

Yet in the same breath we are informed that the same "common people" (subject to mass "delusion and hallucination") managed to thwart the Plan at a number of important junctures—for example, in the 1980 primary election defeat of "the ultimate insider" George Bush, not to mention his failed reelection bid in 1992.

A Syllabus of Errors

In attempting to bolster the theory that the world is controlled by an invisible conspiratorial elite, Marrs throws in everything but the kitchen sink. Thus the timeworn conspiracy theories about the assassination of President John F. Kennedy are trotted out for our perusal. In a novel twist, he implicates George Bush, stating that "his role in the JFK assassination especially deserves scrutiny" (p. 61).

Bush is suspect because of his brief stint as director of the Central Intelligence Agency in the late 1970s. Lest anyone imagine that serving with the CIA puts one beyond the reach of the conspiracy, Marrs makes this claim:

> With their control of such powerful institutions as international banks, national government office-holders, the giant foundations, and the CIA, KGB, and other intelligence agencies, and considering their close working relationships with the Mafia and the drug cartels, the Secret Brotherhood has the capability of either directly or indirectly influencing almost everything that happens to us each minute of our waking and sleeping hours.

> page 126

If such sweeping allegations are true, then no claim is too bizarre for our consideration. Thus the suggestion that Mikhail Gorbachev was actually "a secret agent of the CIA" (p. 103).[6] No person or group is beyond suspicion. Named in a long list of organizations said to be "affiliated with the Illuminati" is Alcoholics Anonymous, though it is unclear how this organization contributes to the breakdown of American society.

Also included is a cryptic reference to "some TV evangelists." Marrs does not elaborate, but casts suspicion elsewhere on Pat Robertson of the Christian Broadcasting Network. What is Robertson's crime, despite his own book entitled *The New World Order* that also purports to expose the Illuminati? For starters, Robertson supported Bush's 1992 presidential campaign. And if that were not proof enough, Marrs discloses that Robertson's father was a U.S. senator (pp. 124, 192).

Is there no end to this madness? Are we to believe that well-known Christian television personalities are controlled by the Secret Brotherhood? One need not be in full agreement with everything Pat Robertson does or says to see the absurdity of such logic. All prudence is seemingly thrown to the wind in the attempt to "prove" that the world is controlled by the secret cadre of the Illuminati.

The Central Flaw

In what Marrs considers an unassailable argument, he mentions a New Age directory of "over 1500 networks," as well as *The Yearbook of International Organizations* which lists "25,000 different international groups based in 200 countries" (pp. 116–117). Apparently assuming that every international organization is (for whatever purpose) actually part of the conspiracy, Marrs concludes triumphantly:

For anyone who refuses to believe that there is a conspiracy and that like-minded groups are working closely together to accomplish the same ends, all I can advise is that you please get your head out of the sand. Someone is behind these 25,000 groups.

pages 116–117

There is indeed someone behind the large and growing number of New Age and occult groups in the world today—none other than the evil one, whom the Bible calls Satan, and the demonic forces under his command:

For our struggle is not against flesh and blood, but against the rulers, against the authorities, against the powers of this dark world and against the spiritual forces of evil in the heavenly realms.

Ephesians 6:12

Note the apostle Paul is saying that the cosmic struggle of the Christian is *not* against flesh and blood, but against spiritual forces of evil. And thus we have the central flaw of conspiracy theories: the attempt to give the conspiracy a physical, earthbound locus, to postulate a group of nine or ten men somewhere on the planet who are actually controlling the world, while Scripture tells us that the central stronghold of our enemy is from another realm altogether.

Obviously the devil does use humans for his evil purposes—men and women in positions of power and authority, as well as organizations dedicated to the overthrow of Christian influence in society. Moreover, just as the Illuminati existed in eighteenth-century Bavaria, subversive organizations doubtless exist today with equally diabolical aims. And I have no doubt that many of those in a position of influence, including politicians, businessmen, educators, scientists, academics, entertainers and those who control our access to news and information, exhibit a thinly disguised contempt for Christianity. This is why many of the details presented in *Dark Majesty* hit the nail on the head. But—and this is a very big but—the book fails in its assertion that all those in positions of influence are *inter-connected* in a flesh-and-blood conspiracy.

A well-known objection to the theory of evolution is that of "missing links" between the various species. It is not sufficient, in other words, to present separate links and postulate that an evolutionary connection exists between them. Thus it is ironic that Christians who recognize this serious flaw in evolutionary theory sometimes fail to apply the same logic to conspiracy theory. The mere presentation of information about individuals and organizations who are hostile to Christianity does not prove the existence of an integrated worldwide conspiracy.

For all its superficially impressive 288 pages, *Dark Majesty* does not name a single individual at the center of the alleged Secret Brotherhood or Illuminati; nor are we told in concrete terms exactly how this inner cadre actually governs the worldwide conspiracy. In short, where are the links?

The available evidence suggests that many disparate New Age and occult individuals do cooperate to a certain extent, depending on how advantageous they deem such cooperation to be. Some collaborate to a substantial degree, while others pursue their aims and purposes independent of like-minded organizations. (Some of them are at each other's throats.)

Dark Majesty, following standard conspiracy arguments, provides no convincing evidence to prove anything beyond this.

But What's the Harm?

One final question should be addressed: What is so harmful about informing people about sinister plots abroad in the world, even if they do not represent an organized conspiracy led by the Secret Brotherhood?

It is constructive, of course, to inform people about demonically inspired schemes that oppose Christianity and its influence in the world. For what purpose? So that, above all, Christians can pray and engage in spiritual warfare. Returning to our passage in Ephesians, we are instructed to "put on the full armor of God":

> Stand firm then, with the belt of truth buckled around your waist, with the breastplate of righteousness in place, and with your feet fitted with the readiness that comes from the gospel of peace. In addition to all this, take up the shield of faith, with which you can extinguish all the flaming arrows of the evil one. Take the helmet of salvation and the sword of the Spirit, which is the word of God. And pray in the Spirit on all occasions with all kinds of prayers and requests. With this in mind, be alert and always keep on praying for all the saints.
>
> Ephesians 6:14–18

God's prescription for conducting spiritual warfare against the forces of evil—Satan and his demonic minions—is "[being] strong in the Lord and in the power of His might" (KJV). This is the only battle plan that will succeed in the face of the withering attacks of the evil one.

How disappointing, then, to find so little emphasis on spiritual warfare in a book that purports to expose the comprehensive satanic plan for planet earth! *Dark Majesty* is permeated with a cynical air of inevitable defeat. One waits in vain for a shout of victory in Christ. And the book ends as gloomily as it begins, leaving the reader with little hope.

What is the harm? In another context Marrs, quoting from a book on alchemy, has unwittingly provided an incisive comment on the obsession with world conspiracy theories:

> Difficult and narrow is the way, and many are those who stray into wrong paths, where they are to find only deceit, error, and falsehood, which will only beguile them into expending vast sums in sheer waste. . . .
>
> page 127

Like the alchemist of old, driven by hopes of fabulous wealth, the fruitless quest for hidden conspiracies will yield only fool's gold.

Notes

Introduction: Nine Peculiar Aircraft

1. Pierre Lagrange, "It Seems Impossible But There It Is," in *Phenomenon: Forty Years of Flying Saucers,* John Spencer and Hilary Evans, eds. (New York: Avon Books, 1988), p. 27.

2. Jacques Vallee, *Confrontations: A Scientist's Search for Alien Contact* (New York: Ballantine Books, 1990), p. 139.

Chapter 1: A Bat Out of Hell

1. "Scientists Dig 9-Mile-Deep Hole and Claim: 'We Drilled through the Gates of Hell,'" *Weekly World News,* April 24, 1990.

2. Rich Buhler, "Scientists Discover Hell in Siberia," *Christianity Today,* July 16, 1990, pp. 28–29. Buhler attempts to track down the Siberian drill site story and makes light of a Norwegian man who fabricated a letter about the incident. The man wrote his letter *after* he had heard about the Siberian story, however, and thus could not have been the originator of it. Buhler's trail ends somewhere in California, and the question of how the story got there remains unanswered.

Chapter 2: Highway Hallucinations or Angelic Messengers?

1. "Mystery Hitchhiker Will Be Hard To Arrest," *Indianapolis Star,* July 26, 1980, p. 5.

2. Nancy Gibbs, "Angels Among Us," *Time,* December 27, 1993, p. 18.

3. Jan Harold Brunvand, *The Vanishing Hitchhiker: American Urban Legends and Their Meanings* (New York: W. W. Norton & Co., 1981), p. 38.

4. Ibid., pp. 38–39.

5. "Archangel Gabriel Reported Warning of '84 Doomsday," *Indianapolis Star,* October 24, 1982, p. 7.

Chapter 3: Entertaining Angels Unawares

1. This quotation and the following ones are taken from Betty Eadie, *Embraced by the Light* (New York: Bantam Books, 1992).

2. Belief in the preexistence of souls was one of the controversial beliefs of the early Church father Origen, for which he was condemned at the Fifth General Council at Constantinople (A.D. 553).

3. Brigham Young, *Journal of Discourses*, Vol. 1, p. 51.

4. Richard Abanes, "Readers Embrace the Light," *Christianity Today*, March 7, 1994, p. 53.

Chapter 4: We Are Not Alone

1. This quotation and the following ones are taken from Whitley Strieber, *Communion* (New York: Avon Books, 1987).

2. It is worth noting that Strieber's description of these entities is similar in several respects to accounts of other abductees. Numerous accounts have described these beings as emasculated, almost fetus-like, with large, black, almond-shaped eyes. An artist's rendition appears on the cover of Strieber's books *Communion* and *Transformation*.

3. This episode and Strieber's reaction may seem exaggerated. But in the opinion of Walt Andrus, editor of the *Mutual UFO Network Journal*, Strieber's story is "frankly mild" in comparison to numerous other published accounts (telephone conversation with the author, September 9, 1994).

4. Cf. Jacques Vallee, *Revelations: Alien Contact and Human Deception* (New York: Ballantine Books, 1991), p. 265; *Confrontations*, p. 18.

5. British researcher Peter Hough decries the fact that "the Americans have stood firmly by the side of E.T. testimony which does not fit and is often ignored or dismissed" ("The Development of UFO Occupants," *Phenomenon*, p. 114).

6. Ibid., p. 112.

7. John Rimmer, "Evaluating the Abductee Experience," *Phenomenon*, p. 167.

8. The occasional alien does find it necessary to wear a helmet, as reported, for example, in Raymond E. Fowler, *The Watchers: The Secret Design Behind UFO Abduction* (New York: Bantam Books, 1991), p. 151, and Vallee, *Confrontations*, p. 54.

9. Richard Neal, M.D., "Generations of Abductions—A Medical Casebook," *UFO*, Vol. 3, 1988, p. 21.

10. Oddly, others describe this strange operation in exactly the same way—as causing a sensation of an "apple crunching" inside their head (*Communion*, p. 126).

11. Whitley Strieber, *Transformation: The Breakthrough* (New York: Avon Books, 1988), p. 112.

12. Fowler, pp. 21–22.

13. Ibid., p. 227.

14. Budd Hopkins, *Intruders: The Incredible Visitations at Copley Woods* (New York: Ballantine Books, 1987), p. 258.
15. Budd Hopkins, "Investigating the Abductees," *Phenomenon*, pp. 141–142. Hopkins, to his credit, is objective enough to state, "I am the first to admit the sheer absurdity of such ideas . . ."; yet he maintains that "outrageousness doesn't mean untruth."
16. Fowler, p. 195.
17. Vallee, *Confrontations,* p. 17.
18. Vallee, *Revelations,* p. 289.
19. Fowler, p. 357.
20. J. Allen Hynek, quoted in Vallee, *Revelations*, p. 290, italics mine. Hynek's colleague Jacques Vallee concurs, denouncing UFOlogists for accepting only "aliens that originate very far from us" (p. 259).

Chapter 5: The Universe Next Door: Are We Looking in the Wrong Dimension?

1. Dr. Allen Tough, "Extraterrestrial UFOs—Yes or No?", *Phenomenon*, p. 271. Attempts to photograph UFOs often (mysteriously) yield only blurry film or indecipherable points of light, as in the case of a Danish policeman who attempted to photograph "a huge, greyish" UFO in southern Jutland in 1970, with disappointing results (Anders Liljegren and others, "UFOs—A Global Phenomenon," *Phenomenon*, p. 69).
2. Ibid. Some of the photographic attempts come from notoriously unreliable abductees. Galactic traveler George Adamski claims he was given free rein by aliens to photograph both the inside and outside of a UFO spacecraft. But "Adamski's photographic bad luck held; one camera was out of focus, while the other malfunctioned, leaving him with but a single blurry shot" (Dennis Stacy, "The Contactee Era," *Phenomenon*, p. 123).
3. Quoted in Clifford Wilson, *The Alien Agenda* (New York: Signet, 1988), p. 71. The granddaddy of such reports is known as the Roswell Incident, the subject of several UFO investigative books. On July 2, 1947, one or two UFOs are alleged to have crashed north of Roswell, New Mexico. The wreckage and bodies of several aliens are said to have been recovered by the U.S. Air Force and spirited away. Perhaps the real question has nothing to do with the merits of this particular case: With estimates of worldwide sightings ranging in the millions, why do UFO enthusiasts continue to focus on an obscure incident said to have occurred in the New Mexico desert more than four decades ago? Is it because they have no better case with which to make their case for the ETH?
4. Vallee, *Revelations*, p. 9, italics mine.
5. Strieber, *Communion*, pp. 136, 271; *Transformation*, p. 73.
6. This quote and the following ones are taken from Strieber, *Transformation.*

7. The story of Balaam's donkey in Numbers 22, who saw the angel invisible to her master, offers an interesting (though not exact) biblical example of this.

8. Reference is made, for example, to the presence of the beings "everywhere," as well as to the teaching that our existence on earth is a school leading us upward to higher spiritual progression.

9. Frank Smyth, "Whispers of Immortality," Vol. 3, *The Unexplained* (New York: Marshall Cavendish, 1983), p. 419.

10. Jenny Randles, "Living with a Close Encounter," *Phenomenon,* p. 150.

11. Rimmer, p. 157.

12. John G. Fuller, *The Interrupted Journey* (New York: Dell, 1966).

13. Hopkins, *Intruders,* p. 6.

14. Vallee, *Revelations,* p. 266.

15. Fowler, p. xv.

16. John A. Keel, "The People Problem," *Phenomenon,* p. 187.

17. Strieber, *Communion,* p. 26.

18. Whitley Strieber quoted in William Alnor, *UFOs in the New Age* (Grand Rapids: Baker, 1992), p. 105. In *Transformation* (p. 200; acknowledgments) Strieber defends and pays tribute to Salena Fox, high priestess of Wicca (witchcraft).

19. Lynn G. Catoe, *UFOs and Related Subjects: An Annotated Bibliography* (prepared for the USAF Office of Scientific Research), cited in *SCP Journal,* August 1977, and Alnor, p. 148.

20. Mark Moravec, "Is There a UFO State of Mind?", *Phenomenon,* p. 335.

21. Strieber, *Transformation,* p. 69.

22. Strieber, *Transformation,* p. 9.

23. Strieber, *Communion,* pp. 276–277; cf. *Transformation,* pp. 13–14.

24. Strieber, *Transformation,* p. 190.

Chapter 6: Analysis of a Phenomenon

1. Strieber, *Communion,* pp. 139, 141.

2. Vallee, *Revelations,* p. 209.

3. David M. Jacobs, *Secret Life: Firsthand Accounts of UFO Abductions* (New York: Simon & Schuster, 1992), pp. 308–311; John E. Mack, *Abduction: Human Encounters with Aliens* (New York: Charles Scribner's Sons, 1994), pp. 414–417; Edith Fiore, *Encounters: A Psychologist Reveals Case Studies of Abductions by Extraterrestrials* (New York: Doubleday, 1989), pp. 325–331.

4. Vallee, *Revelations,* p. 184.

5. Mack, p. 34.

6. George Riland, *The New Steinerbooks Dictionary of the Paranormal* (New York: Warner Books, 1980), p. 84.

7. David W. Clarke, "Spooklights," *Phenomenon,* p. 313. Vallee concurs that the UFO phenomenon "is associated with a form of nonhuman

consciousness that manipulates space and time in ways we do not understand" (*Revelations*, p. 259).

8. Paul Devereux, "Earthlights," *Phenomenon*, p. 326.

9. Ibid.

10. Stacy, p. 122.

11. Rimmer notes the abduction case of a certain Villas Boas (Brazil, October 1957) who, after being allowed to examine what appeared to be a control room within the UFO, "tried to remove a clock-like item of equipment, but was foiled by his captors" (p. 137).

12. The word *form* is preferable here to *create*. The ability to create, as properly understood, is inappropriate in relation to creatures, and especially demons.

13. Randles, p. 149. Similarly Tough suggests that "one part of our brain may be capable of *creating lifelike experiences* for us at certain times" (p. 269, italics mine).

14. Strieber, *Transformation*, p. 255.

15. Jacobs, pp. 49–50.

16. Strieber, *Transformation*, p. 193. Elsewhere he wonders aloud, "Maybe they are the best friends I could ever have" (p. 141).

17. Mack, pp. 416–417.

18. Mack, p. 422. Lest anyone imagine that such talk is the providence of starry-eyed UFO fanatics gathering on moonlit hilltops for close encounters with UFOs, we should recall that John Mack is a Pulitzer Prize-winning author and Harvard University psychiatrist. The fact that respected authority figures are openly advocating the occult-mystical explanation for UFO phenomena indicates the alarming degree to which Western culture has abandoned the Judeo-Christian worldview of the Bible.

19. Fowler, p. 355.

20. Vallee, *Revelations*, pp. 8–9.

21. Mack, p. 412, italics mine.

22. Raymond E. Fowler, *The Andreasson Affair: Phase Two* (Englewood Cliffs, N.J.: Prentice-Hall, 1982), p. 261.

23. Vallee, *Revelations*, pp. 124–25.

24. Fowler, *Andreasson*, p. 262.

25. Mack, p. 48.

26. Ibid.

27. Eadie, pp. 117–118, 123.

28. Jacobs, p. 307.

29. Vallee, *Confrontations*, p. 177.

Chapter 7: The Mysterious "Organization X"

1. This quotation and the following ones are taken from "Organization X," *The Midnight Cry* (Summerfield, Fla.: reprint, n.d.).

Chapter 8: Antichrist in the Bible

1. See J. R. Church, "Will the Antichrist Be Gay?", *Prophecy in the News,* April 1993, pp. 1–3.

2. This and the following quotes are taken from J. R. Church, "The World Is Looking for a Supernatural, Superhuman Superstar!", *Prophecy in the News,* August 1988, p. 13.

Chapter 9: The Wandering Caesar

1. See Suetonius, *Nero 57;* Tacitus, *History* 1.2; 2.8–9; Dio Cassius 64.9.

2. *Martyrdom and Ascension of Isaiah,* 4.2, in James H. Charlesworth, ed., *The Old Testament Pseudepigrapha,* Vol. 2 (Garden City, N.Y.: Doubleday & Co., 1985), p. 161.

3. See Commentary on Daniel 11:29, cited in William C. Weinrich, "Antichrist in the Early Church," *Concordia Theological Quarterly* (Vol. 49, 1985), p. 140. Cf. I. T. Beckwith: "The association of Nero with Antichrist persisted through the following centuries. Its acceptance by many is well attested; e.g. by Commodianus, c. 250; the commentator Victorinus, c. 300; Sulpicius Severus, about the end of the 4th cent.; Augustine, *De civ. Dei,* c. 426" (*The Apocalpyse of John* [Grand Rapids: Baker, 1967], p. 402n).

4. Sibylline (Christian), I.324ff. Cf. Beckwith, p. 403.

5. Cf. Revelation 9:11: "They had as king over them the angel of the Abyss, whose name in Hebrew is Abaddon, and in Greek, Apollyon"; and Revelation 16:16: "Then they gathered the kings together to the place that in Hebrew is called Armageddon."

6. "Taking the Apocalyptist's picture of the Beast's activity as a whole we can see that he is chiefly interested in foretelling the progress of Satan's warfare with the Church on to the awful culmination in which Satan will work through the mysterious personality of Antichrist. It appears certain that the precise relation of that personality to Nero or any other historic individual is a quite subordinate point in the author's mind" (Beckwith, p. 406).

7. Walter K. Price, *The Coming Antichrist* (Chicago: Moody Press, 1974), p. 150.

8. Eusebius, *Ecclesiastical History,* 3.25.1–3.

9. Quoted in Eusebius, 3.25.4.

Chapter 10: The King of France

1. Ernest R. Sandeen, *The Roots of Fundamentalism: British and American Millennarianism, 1800–1930* (Chicago: University of Chicago Press, 1970), pp. 6–7. Quoted in Dwight Wilson, *Armageddon Now!* (Grand Rapids: Baker Book House, 1977), p. 19.

2. Sandeen, p. 6, quoted in Wilson, p. 19.

3. George Stanley Faber, *A Dissertation on the Prophecies, That Have Been Fulfilled, Are Now Fulfilling, or Will Hereafter Be Fulfilled, Rela-*

tive to the Great Period of 1260 Years; the Papal and Mohammedan Apostasies; the Tyrannical Reign of Antichrist, or the Infidel Power; and the Restoration of the Jews, Second Edition (New York: M. and W. Ward and Evert Duyckinck, 1811); and *A General and Connected View of the Prophecies Relative to the Conversion, Restoration, Union, and Future Glory of the Houses of Judah and Israel; the Progress and Final Overthrow of the Antichristian Confederacy in the Land of Palestine; and the Ultimate General Diffusion of Christianity* (Boston: William Andrews, 1809).

Chapter 11: The Fettuccine Fascist

1. Arno C. Gaebelein, *Our Hope* 39 (1933), pp. 548–549, quoted in James Alan Patterson, "Changing Images of the Beast: Apocalyptic Conspiracy Theories in American History," *Journal of the Evangelical Theological Society* 31 (December 1988), p. 450.

2. W. Percy Hicks, "Proposed Revival of the Old Roman Empire," *The Pentecostal Evangel,* March 20, 1926, p. 4, quoted in Wilson, p. 83.

3. Wilson, p. 83.

4. Oswald J. Smith, "Is the Antichrist at Hand?" (tract, n.d.), quoted in Price, p. 39.

5. Harry A. Ironside quoted in Price, p. 40. Cf. William S. McBirnie, *What the Bible Says About Mussolini* (Norfolk, Va.: McBirnie Publications Association, 1944). McBirnie listed 44 prophecies allegedly fulfilled by Mussolini.

6. Timothy P. Weber, *Living in the Shadow of the Second Coming* (Grand Rapids: Zondervan, 1983), p. 179.

7. Ibid., p. 80.

Chapter 12: The Lord of East End

1. Saint Ephrem, "Discourse of S. Ephrem on the Antichrist II," 138B, quoted in Wilhelm Bousset, *The Antichrist Legend: A Chapter in Christian and Jewish Folklore* (London: Hutchinson & Co, 1896), p. 191.

2. Benjamin Creme, *Messages from Maitreya the Christ,* Vol. 1 (London: Tara Press, 1980), pp. 16–17, quoted in Albert James Dager, "Is Anti-christ Here?", *Media Spotlight* Special Report (Santa Ana, Cal.: Media Spotlight Ministries, 1982), p. 6.

3. J. R. Church, "The Christ is Here," *Prophecy in the News* 2, May 1982, p. 13. The following also present Maitreya as a possible Antichrist: J. R. Church, "The Christ Wasn't There!", *Prophecy in the News* 2, October 1982, pp. 1–2; J. R. Church, "The Tara Center is at it Again!", *Prophecy in the News* 7, February 1987, p. 1; Troy Lawrence (pseud.), "New Age 'Messiah' Identified," *Prophecy in the News* 8, October 1988, pp. 14–16; Ralph G. Griffin, "The Christ is in the World," *Prophecy in the News* 10, July 1990, pp. 5, 13; N. W. Hutchings, "Is Maitreya the Antichrist?", *The Gospel Truth* 22, July 1982, pp. 1–4; David F. Webber, "New Age Pentecost," *The Gospel Truth* 28, January 1987, pp. 1–3.

4. Constance Cumby, "Maitreya: The New Age Messiah," *The Hidden Dangers of the Rainbow* (Shreveport, La.: Huntington House, 1982), p. 19.

5. This quotation and the following ones are taken from Jeane Dixon, *My Life and Prophecies* (New York: William Morrow, 1969).

6. Troy Lawrence, *The New Age Messiah Identified* (Lafayette, La.: Huntington House, 1991), cover.

7. Ibid.

8. B. M. Ahmad, *Ahmadiyya Movement* (n.p., n.d.), pp. 3–4, quoted in *Prophecy in the News* 8, October 1988, p. 14. Note: No further publishing information is given in the article concerning *Ahmadiyya Movement*.

9. Lawrence, pp. 161–162.

10. Author's phone conversation with the secretary-receptionist at Huntington House in Lafayette, Louisiana, on February 9, 1995.

11. Troy Lawrence, "Solving the Mystery" (n.p., n.d.). Faxed to me on February 9, 1995, from the office of Emissary Publications, Clackamas, Oregon.

12. Erik Pement, "Troy Lawrence Identified," *Cornerstone*, Vol. 20, No. 95, 1991, pp. 16, 24. Cf. book review of Troy Lawrence's *New Age Messiah Identified* in *Christian Research Newsletter*, September–October 1991, p. 3.

13. Charles R. Taylor, *The Antichrist King—Juan Carlos* (Huntington Beach, Cal.: Today in Bible Prophecy, Inc., 1993), p. 1.

14. Jack Van Impe, *Jack Van Impe Ministries International Newsletter*, June 22, 1994.

Chapter 13: Just a Footstep Away

1. Fowler, *Watchers*, p. xiii.

2. Fowler, *Andreasson*, p. 2.

3. Ibid., p. 87.

4. Ibid.

5. Fowler, *Watchers*, p. 39.

6. Ibid., p. 374.

7. Ibid.

8. Fowler, *Andreasson*, p. 257.

9. Ibid., p. 258.

10. Strieber, *Communion*, pp. 282–283. The two sides of *yin-yang* do not refer to good and evil, as some in the West suppose; this would wrongly impose a Christian interpretation. Taoism, like all Eastern thought, does not admit the absolute existence of evil. Rather, its adherents believe that seemingly negative experiences have their purpose in leading men toward enlightenment.

11. Quoted in Fowler, *Andreasson*, pp. 8–9.

12. Mack, *Abduction*, p. 412.

Chapter 14: Keep Looking Up!

1. Strieber, *Communion*, p. 76.
2. Stuart Goldman, unpublished manuscript, quoted in Alnor, p. 43.
3. I am indebted for the following insights, which have been adapted from *Victory Miracle Living* (San Diego: Morris Cerullo World Evangelism, January 1994), pp. 27–31.
4. Marilynn Carlson Webber, *A Rustle of Angels* (Grand Rapids: Zondervan, 1994), p. 77.
5. Ibid., p. 78.

Appendix: A Review of Texe Marrs' *Dark Majesty*

1. This quotation and the following ones from Texe Marrs are taken from *Dark Majesty* (Austin, Tex.: Living Truth Publishers, 1992).
2. Y. Jonathan Glover, *What Sort of People Should There Be?* (New York: Penguin Books, 1984), no page number given; quoted in Marrs, p. 236.
3. John Barron, *The KGB Today: The Hidden Hand* (Pleasantville, N.Y.: Reader's Digest Press), no page number given; quoted in Marrs, p. 253.
4. *Christian Awareness Newsletter,* Summer/Fall 1991, p. 10; quoted in Marrs, p. 269.
5. Elsewhere Reagan is presented as part of the conspiracy. Commenting on the 1988 Republican convention, Marrs writes: "If Satan himself had written the speeches of George Bush and Ronald Reagan at the Republican National Convention in 1988 in New Orleans, he could not have done a better job. President Reagan, a 33rd-degree honorary Mason who is often called the great communicator, charmed the vast audience with his illuminist-laden talk" (p. 95).
6. Marrs, while careful not to commit himself to this possibility, nevertheless asserts, "I believe it is extremely possible that this is the case."